D0374656

CASES IN INTERNATIONAL POLITICS
David V. Edwards, *General Editor*

INTERNATIONAL COMMUNITY
A Regional and
Global Study

Roger W. Cobb
and
Charles Elder

University of Pennsylvania

HOLT, RINEHART AND WINSTON, INC.
New York   Chicago   San Francisco   Atlanta
Dallas   Montreal   Toronto   London   Sydney

INTERNATIONAL COMMUNITY

A Regional and

Global Study

International Community: A Regional and Global Study
by Roger W. Cobb and Charles Elder
Copyright © 1970 by Holt, Rinehart and Winston, Inc.
Library of Congress Catalog Card Number: 77-115175
SBN: 03-081157-0
Printed in the United States of America
1 2 3 4 5 6 7 8 9

Preface

This book was developed with the purpose of achieving four major objectives. First, our desire was to systematically consider the sources of what might be called integration theory at the nation-state level. Where in political science and associated disciplines have the antecedents of integration been developed, and how do they relate to the literature on community formation at the international level? To answer that question, we have focused not only on the substantive literature of research findings but on the major approaches to the study of community development such as the systems and aggregative perspectives.

A second objective was to provide a general model, or framework, which would give the reader an overall perspective for interrelating existing studies on community development. In this instance, a wide variety of sources of integration were considered from attitudes or common values to various forms of communication both at the private, or nongovernmental, level and between governments. An attempt was made to show where the various approaches to the study of integration have overlapped and the extent to which one aspect of community formation might be highly correlated with another indicator of integration.

A third objective was to provide a study which focused on more than one level of nation-state alignment. That is, most studies of integration have emphasized a particular area of the world and have ventured no further. Our aim was to take such a region and then compare that area with the global pattern of country alignments. To accomplish that end, we have gathered data on a variety of integrative indicators from mass attitudes toward other countries to a variety of transaction measures including trade, mail, telephone calls, tourism, and student exchange. We have examined this set of indicators for a sample of fourteen countries in the North Atlantic area over a period of twelve years, from 1952 to 1964. In addition, we have focused on virtually the same set of indicators for forty-nine countries throughout the world for the year 1955.

In this context, two caveats are in order concerning our approach to the study of integration. The term has a great many conceptual and operational definitions, and our approach was not to cover all such possibilities, but to review some of the most prominent ones. In this context, we emphasize that no single operational definition necessarily provides an index of a concept such as integration. An operational definition is but one measure of a concept. Doubtless, there are other approaches which may not have been covered.

Secondly, a word is in order concerning the methodology used to test propositions. Our emphasis was on the use of multivariate techniques, primarily canonical correlational analysis. For those who prefer simple correlations, such matrices are provided in the text.

Our perspective in the study was an ecological one, as we have looked for general trends in alignment patterns. Our objective was not to explain every variation that exists, but merely to isolate patterns in the complex world of alignment patterns. One of the key questions to which we have addressed ourselves is the extent to which efforts to develop integration at the regional level are complementary, or antithetical to, developments of community at the global level.

Finally, we have sought to introduce the reader to a more rigorous study of integration utilizing propositions which could be tested with data, rather than anecdotes. We have developed a set of propositions which can be subjected to an empirical verification with a stringent set of methodological procedures. It is hoped that more precise research designs will become prevalent in the future, so that speculations about trends in regional or world communities can be scrutinized in the light of empirical inquiry.

R. W. C.
C. E.

Philadelphia, Pa.
January 1970

Acknowledgments

This project was truly a joint enterprise in every sense of the word. While the genesis of the study involved two dissertation efforts, the material was gathered in a framework developed jointly by the authors. The creation of the model, research of relevant hypotheses, data collection, and empirical analysis were all aspects of the joint effort. Attribution of a name to a specific chapter, common in joint enterprises, is not possible in this context, since both authors participated in the drafting and revising of each of the chapters.

Several people made a contribution to the completion of the project. The authors would like to thank Professors Lee Anderson and Kenneth Janda, who served as the advisors of the project and provided aid and advice whenever needed.

Professor Philip Hastings of the Roper Public Opinion Center in Williamstown, Massachusetts, was helpful in making relevant data available to the authors.

The authors would like to acknowledge a special debt owed to Professor Harold Guetzkow, who sustained both of their graduate careers and was partially responsible for the inception of this study. Without his aid and perspicacity, this study would not have been completed. Through his Simulated International Process (SIP) project at Northwestern University, he provided financial assistance in the procurement of needed data sources compiled by various international organizations. In addition, he provided financial aid to allow the use of two research assistants, Susan Weissblatt and Robert Piepmeier, who helped in the drudgeries of key punching and data processing to prepare analysis decks.

Several people were helpful in data collection, particularly in gathering relevant transaction information. A special thanks is given to the anonymous officials of government bodies, particularly those in national post offices, who aided immeasurably in the reporting of mail flow data and filling in gaps existing in publications of mail exchange by the Universal Postal Union. In addition, Paul Smoker, a Research Associate affiliated with the SIP project at Northwestern, was of assistance in providing many helpful suggestions on the gathering and procurement of relevant data; and he also participated in field excursions to relevant sites in gathering data. Finally, Professor Chadwick Alger obtained many relevant documents from specialized agencies in Geneva, Switzerland, during his stay there in the academic year of 1966–1967.

Contents

Table of Propositions

PART I

INTEGRATION THEORY AND COMMUNITY DEVELOPMENT

chapter 1

Community Formation
in the International System

Introduction: A One of the principal developments in the
Specific Instance of post–World War II milieu has been the crea-
Community Creation tion of a series of supranational regional communities in various areas of the world. This
can be seen in the growth of a group of multilateral alliances in the
military sphere to the establishment of a series of free-trade areas from
Western Europe to Latin America.

The most notable success has been the surge of integrative activity
in Western Europe. Rising from the shambles of World War II, there are
now several institutions accelerating cooperation across national boundaries from the European Economic Community to the North Atlantic
Treaty Organization. The consequences of regional unification have been
beneficial for the member states. Within five years after the creation of
the Common Market, trade among the six members had increased by
85 percent over the level prior to its inception and the gross national
product for the group had increased by 33 percent (Etzioni, 1965, 230).[1]

Despite the rapid economic and military recovery, Western Europe
is now beset with a series of policy disputes. Disagreements have arisen
between two of the chief protagonists, Britain and France, with a policy
split between France and the United States, the latter being responsible
for rebuilding Western Europe in the last two decades (Spanier, 1967).

1. The member states of the Common Market are Belgium, France, Italy, Luxembourg, the Netherlands, and the German Federal Republic (West Germany).

A More General Problem   The foregoing analysis reflects a typical commentary on some of the developments in the past two decades. However, such a perspective is concerned with a basic problem confronting political analysts: the development of supranational communities in a world where national prerogatives have been carefully guarded. The general theoretical questions associated with the processes of community formation—the process through which inter-unit bonds develop to give structure and stability to larger social collectivities—are among the most persistent and rudimentary problems of political analysis.

Contemporary social and political developments have, however, thrust these questions into a new prominence and have given them a special urgency. At all levels of political organization, the erstwhile familiar landscape is eroding. At the local level, the rapid growth of urbanization has generated countless new problems of coordination and control—problems which seem impervious to, if not exacerbated by, the anachronistic forms of political organization left to cope with them. At the societal level, the proliferation of national political entities has left the bulk of the world's population to grope with the prodigious problems of transforming fragmented traditional societies into modern nation-states. Internationally, modern technology and weaponry have created a global interdependence that precariously hangs on little more than a common fear of annihilation.

The challenges posed by these developments have betrayed rather ingloriously the meagerness of our knowledge of the processes of creating and sustaining viable social relationships. How, why, and under what conditions do the relatively ordered and stable patterns of community relations emerge between social entities? These are indeed perplexing questions, questions without clear answers. Yet they are important questions, for these patterns of social interaction are what eventually come to characterize and define the structure of larger social systems.

This study attempts to come to grips with some of these problems. The specific focus is on the international system and on factors presumed relevant to the creation of a more viable international community. According to Karl W. Deutsch (1954),

> The fundamental problem of international politics and organization is the creation of conditions under which stable peaceful relations among nation states are possible and likely. Ultimately each nation's security must be assured through the existence of a community embracing all nations [33].

In order to reduce this problem to manageable proportions and to promote the creation of the community Deutsch envisions, there is a clear need for more explicit identification of those conditions which foster or facilitate international cooperation.

Impressive progress has been made toward this end. Recent conceptual and theoretical developments, particularly in the areas of communication theory and general systems analysis, have provided valuable insights into the general conditions necessary to create and sustain interunit bonds. Perhaps even more importantly, this work offers a useful paradigm for further systematic exploration of the problem. For despite the great strides forward, it remains the case that except in the most abstract and general terms, the task of explicitly identifying the factors which promote or impede collaborative relations between nations has only begun.

Work in the area has not, however, suffered for want of variables. In fact, one finds within the recent literature a plethora of factors being cited as potentially important. Elegant and often compelling arguments can be found for the significance of almost all of these variables as wellsprings of international cooperation. Unfortunately, for one plausible assertion, there often exists another equally plausible proposition contradicting it. Moreover, cases can generally be found as evidence for whichever contention one chooses to support.

Of this multitude of allegedly important factors, which are in fact important in the relations between nations? What is their relative importance vis-à-vis one another? And what kind of sequential relationships exist among them? These are hard questions, all of which largely remain to be answered. Neither abstract theorizing nor common sense has been able to resolve these problems satisfactorily. Clearly, recourse must be sought through rigorous empirical inquiry.

The Problem of Community Formation Within the Context of Research in International Relations   As a field of study, international relations encompasses a broad range of phenomena. Cognizant of the complex web of interrelated factors with which they must deal, international relations scholars have been understandably reluctant to reduce their inquiry to a simple set of explanatory propositions, or hypotheses. As a result, work within the field has tended to be largely impressionistic description and evaluation. Only recently has a premium been placed on the sort of conceptual clarity and refinement of focus necessary for systematic analysis. Behavioral propositions explicitly linking one set of variables to another are still relatively rare. Nonetheless, the international relations literature remains a rich source for insights regarding the influences which may condition and shape the course of international affairs, even though one is often left to his own devices to give operational meaning and content to the assertions this literature contains.

Collectively, those factors which are said to influence the pattern of inter-nation relationships may be called background variables. Presumably, these are the wellsprings of specific inter-nation relationships. They fall roughly into three categories: (1) properties of the geophysical environment; (2) subsystemic, or unit, properties (i.e., internal sociopolitical properties of nations themselves); and (3) systemic properties (i.e., characteristics of configurations of nations considered collectively). These may be seen as analytically distinct sets of explanatory or independent variables. A distinct tradition has been associated with each set in the study of international relations.

Traditional Views of Background Variables Despite its great diversity, most current work in international relations may be classified in terms of one of two leading traditions—the first actor-, or subsystemically, oriented; the other systemic in orientation. After enjoying considerable prominence in the 1930s and 40s, a third tradition (the geopolitical school) has largely decayed. Dismembered elements of this tradition can now be found in the field of geography and the remaining two traditions in international relations. The exaggerated claims of geopoliticians such as Mackinder are today ignored. More modest claims for the importance of geography as a determinant of international behavior are now made by students of both the subsystemic, or actor-oriented, tradition and the systemic tradition. The former typically find geography to be either a determinant of national power (Organski 1958) or a motivational influence on national decision-makers (Sprout and Sprout, 1956). Systemically oriented scholars, on the other hand, are inclined to view geography as a natural constraint on patterns of interaction (Linnemann, 1966) or as a strategic consideration influencing the patterns of coalition formation (Liska, 1962).

With the demise of the geopolitical school, the prevailing traditions in the field of international relations are now distinguished largely by the level of analysis at which study is concentrated (Sondermann, 1961). Following Singer (1961), we have characterized these as systemic and subsystemic. As Singer points out, each involves a definite perspective; and each has its theoretical assets and liabilities. Rather clearly, the kinds of questions asked at each level differ. Inquiry at the subsystemic level is directed toward understanding what internal characteristics and processes are relevant to a nation's external behavior and how. At the systemic level, the basic question centers on how the international system, qua system, works.

Thus, within the subsystemic, or actor-oriented, tradition, one finds such substantive foci as the study of foreign policy (Snyder, Bruck, and Sapin, 1962) and assessments of the impact of national characteristics and capabilities on external behavior (Rummel, 1968). The former focus has tended to be phenomenological in approach; the latter ecological.

Within the systemic tradition, the locus of analysis shifts from national characteristics and actions to patterns of interaction. Work within this tradition has centered primarily on the abstract description and evaluation of alternative possible international systems. These include the classic notions of balance and imbalance as well as a variety of proposals for world organization (Kaplan, 1957). Among the more recent contributions, however, are efforts directed toward the systematic analysis of transaction flows (Deutsch and Savage, 1966; 1967).

As indicated earlier, students working within these traditions have evinced little concern for explicitly delineating independent and dependent variables. In general, the dependent variable most frequently seems to be externally directed national behavior, the independent variables being drawn from one or more of the three sets of background factors discussed above. Exception to this is sometimes found in studies of the systemic orientation. To explain alterations, or transformations, of the international system, the actions of a state may be posited as a disturbing influence necessitating systemic readjustment. In this case, the independent variable is the action of a nation and the dependent variable the relational patterns between nations.

The tack taken in this study bears semblances to both of these explanatory orientations, but is directed toward a different set of linkages. An effort is made to relate background variables of the three types—geophysical, subsystemic, and systemic—not to national actions, but directly to patterns of international interaction and collaboration. The logic for redirecting analysis in this fashion comes from several sources, most importantly from communications theory.

The Contribution of Communications Theory to the Study of Inter-Nation Collaboration   Communications theory has provided a framework for and has given impetus to a major contemporary thrust in international relations research (viz., the study of international integration). In speaking of communications theory, however, it must be noted that the word "theory" is used rather loosely. Deutsch (1963), whose genius is in large part responsible for its development, points out that what is involved is not a full-fledged theory, but a point of view, a way of viewing complex systems.

The specific notions from communications theory of relevance here are fairly simple and straightforward. Nonetheless, they have important research implications in terms of design and analysis. The basic argument stems from four elementary observations.

First, relationships between social units are created and sustained through communication. Wiener has expressed the matter thus, "Communication is the cement that makes organizations. Communication alone enables a group to think together, to see together, and to act together" (in Deutsch, 1963, 77).

The second observation notes that communication involves certain loads, or burdens, for the communication units. The costs of communication tax both the capabilities and the attention of the units involved. Therefore, for effective relations to be maintained, capabilities and attention must be at least commensurate with the level of communication load (Deutsch, 1954, 1963; Deutsch et al., 1957; Russett, 1963, 1965).

The relevant capabilities are of two varieties. The first, which Russett (1963) has called the capacity to act, is primarily dependent upon the administrative and material capabilities of the participating units. The second, which might be called the capacity to interact, presumes not only a common capacity to act but also sufficient mutuality of identification and perspective to allow meaningful communication to occur. Thus, political, social, and cultural properties of the communicating units become important. The two types of capabilities are to some extent overlapping and inherently complementary. For example, the socioeconomic development of a country may not only enhance its capacity to act but also provide interests and perspectives that will facilitate interaction with other socioeconomically developed nations. The point is simply that both types of capabilities are essential to effective intercourse.

The third basic notion from communications theory is the idea that "transactions flow . . . establish[es] mutual relevance of actors. An actor with whom you have very much to do is relevant to you" (Deutsch, 1964a, 67). In more general form, the assumption is, "The higher the transaction levels between two groups, the more salient each becomes to the other . . ." (Toscano, 1964, 101). Given this assumption, the level of interaction, or transaction, between the members of two social units may be taken as a behavioral measure of their mutual relevance.

There are, of course, multifarious channels of intercourse. No one measure is likely to be sufficient to indicate the mutual relevance of two units. Rather, what is more likely of importance is the mutually reinforcing pattern of a multiplicity of relational channels (Deutsch, 1966). Thus, in no case . . . must the basic fact of multidimensionality be forgotten. All ranges of transaction, and all the characteristics of any one range, have full meaning only in the context of the ensemble of at least several other major ranges that characterize the transaction flows between the participating populations as a whole [Deutsch, 1954, 59].

The fourth and final observation from communications theory relates to the institutionalization of patterns of mutual relevance. The fact that patterns of interaction and transaction flows may be taken as indicators of mutual relevance does not mean they are necessarily pleasant or beneficial or that they are free from conflict. But, as Deutsch (1964a) observes, "The one thing which is unlikely to accompany a high level of transaction is continued high tension and conflict. . ." (67). To understand the reasoning here, we must go back to the arguments relating to loads and capabilities.

It has been observed that communication (i.e., interaction, or transaction) carries certain burdens for the units involved. To meet the mutual problems created by the processes of communicating and interacting, these units may establish standards, or formal procedures, for coordination and control. The need for such formal arrangements will, of course, increase with the level of communication load.

In sum, these arguments from communications theory suggest a clear linkage between background variables and patterns of inter-nation interaction and collaboration. The various types of background factors provide an indication of the relative costs of interaction and allow us to assess the mutuality of capabilities and interest of two nations. Thus, the behavioral patterns of mutual relevance between nations may be considered a function of these background variables. Mutual relevance, in turn, will enhance the probability of formal collaborative arrangements arising between nations.

The Contribution of Field Theory to the Study of Inter-Nation Collaboration Before proceeding further, it is incumbent upon us to note another area of theoretical development, namely, social field theory. Although less frequently cited, field theory offers a perspective somewhat parallel and complementary to that of communications theory.

To understand field theory, one may start with the commonplace observation that homogeneity promotes intercourse, an idea aptly expressed in the folk saw, Birds of a feather flock together. Such homogeneity, of course, refers to a given set of background properties. March and Simon provide the formal hypothesis: "The greater the homogeneity in *background*, the greater the frequency of interaction" (63). Etzioni

(1965) notes, however, that "not all background characteristics are of the same relevance. . ." (19). Nor, for that matter, is it necessarily the case that heterogeneity will be destructive to intercourse. Heterogeneity may, in fact, promote interaction, as is duly noted in the aphorism, Opposites attract. Furthermore, as has been previously suggested, no single background trait need be as important as the configuration, or pattern, formed by a variety of background elements considered collectively.

These notions, particularly the idea that the "distance" or "closeness" between two social units somehow affect their relationship, are replete throughout the social sciences. They find their paradigmatic expression, however, in what has been called social field theory. Its philosophical bases were outlined in the 1930's and 40's by Lewin. Like communications theory, field theory is not a theory in the usual sense of the term. Its contribution is essentially a perspective. Or as Lewin suggests, "Field theory is probably best characterized as a method of analyzing causal relations and of building scientific constructs" (45).

The method is founded on two basic premises. First, to understand or to predict the behavior of a social unit, the unit and its environment have to be considered as one constellation of interdependent factors. Lewin terms this totality of factors the "life space," or "social field," of that unit. Secondly, the behavior of the unit may be viewed as a simple function of its life space (i.e., its relative position within the ecological setting which defines the field).

Wright has been primarily responsible for the development of field theory in international relations. In his 1942 classic *A Study of War*, he writes:

> Is it possible to develop an analysis more adequate than those of the past for dealing with war in our time? Such analysis should, in a single formula, relate the factors emphasized in each of the points of view about war (i.e., technological, legal, sociological, and psychological). Factors inherent in a given period of history may be called "distances" between states, and factors dependent on the decisions of actors may be called "policies." It may be assumed as a first approximation that the probability of war is a function of the distances between states and of the policies which they pursue (332).

Wright (1955) has subsequently elaborated and refined these ideas to allow for analyses of relationships other than war.

The verbally structured conceptions of Lewin and Wright have recently been given more formal mathematical structure by Rummel (1965). Rummel's field conception divides social reality into unit attributes and inter-unit behaviors, each of which defines a vector space.

Within the attribute space, each social unit is located as a vector in terms of its attributes. Within the behavior space, every pair of social units, called a dyad, is located as a vector in accordance with the interaction of the two members . . . [T]he dyad vector in behavioral space is a vector function of the configuration of social unit vectors in attribute space. The function . . . is based on defining a distance vector in attribute space which connects the social unit vectors. The notion is that the nature of the distance between two social units on their attributes is a force determining their behavior toward each other [184–185].

It may be observed that the variables defining unit attributes in social field theory correspond rather closely with those used to define unit capabilities in communications theory. But while communications theory tends to emphasize the level, or magnitude, of these attributes or capabilities, field theory directs our attention to their comparability or similarity, thus underscoring the importance of what we have called the capacity to interact.

chapter 2

Approaches to the Study of Community Integration

A Key Concept The general perspective contributed by students of communications and field theory serves as the basis for a substantial body of recent literature in international relations. Sparked by the post–World War II developments in Western Europe, this literature consists primarily of case studies and theoretical assessments of the prospects for international integration or unification among selected nations. This literature serves as an important source for the specific hypotheses outlined in Chapter 3. There we will extrapolate rather freely from the work of a number of scholars. Like much of the international relations literature, work in this area continues to suffer from a lack of clarity regarding independent and dependent variables. The core concept, integration, is itself a major source of confusion. As Jacob and Teune have observed, "The concept of integration, though widely used to describe closely knit political and economic relationships, has not been precisely and consistently defined even in some of the important research and statements of public policy concerning it" (14). Nonetheless, an examination of the general approaches to the study of integration in the range of phenomena that have been studied under this rubric can be instructive.

A Classification of Integration Studies   What are the general approaches to the study of integration? Deutsch and his associates (1957) focus on the North Atlantic area as the region most conducive to community formation.[1] They examine the bases of political cohesion over the last three centuries and isolate the key components. They posit a minimal condition for a political community: the likelihood that violence will not be used as a means for resolving conflicts. Any area which has fulfilled this criterion, they say, is "integrated" as a "security-community."

Assuming the crucial significance of the security community, what are the requisites which will produce greater cohesion among states? Deutsch and his colleagues (1957, 44–53) posit two key elements on the basis of a review of trends over three centuries. First, a congruence on major values among the subunits is necessary for the ensuing development of a community. A second requirement is mutual responsiveness, which entails constant contact among the community members. They find that one factor of alleged importance, external threat, is not conducive to community formation; the threat of an enemy leads to certain cooperative efforts over the short run, but is not essential in an enduring commitment to a security community.

Deutsch and his associates (1957, 5–8, 79–83) draw a further distinction between types of security communities, as states which merge formally into a new unit are classified as "amalgamated security communities." This phenomenon is rather scarce in their investigation, a prime example being the union of Scotland and England in 1707. A more common occurrence is the existence of a group of states retaining their independent governmental structures, but interacting in an atmosphere where violence is not considered as a possible alternative in resolving conflicts. Such groupings, or "pluralistic security communities," fulfill the first definition of integration posited above. A pluralistic security-community has been a more viable entity in promoting peaceful relations in the past than amalgamation, which was subject to fragmentation, they observe.

Can most regions be described as integrated, using an absence of

1. The countries included in Deutsch's study of the North Atlantic area are Austria, Belgium, Canada, Denmark, Finland, France, West Germany, Iceland, Ireland, Italy, Luxembourg, the Netherlands, Norway, Portugal, Spain, Sweden, Switzerland, the United Kingdom, and the United States.

Deutsch chose this area because only the North Atlantic countries exemplified the notion of a "core area," or nucleus, for ensuing attempts at developing cohesion. Primarily the notion revolves around industrial capacity with the economic potential of France, West Germany, and the United States cited as being the basis of success in developing cohesion.

conflict in settling disputes as the indicator? This criterion would not apply to most areas of the world, as violence is a characteristic of the modern political scene (Wright). Frequency of conflict was useful in classifying relations among European states over the last three centuries, but peaceful relations have been achieved in the North Atlantic area since 1945. What are alternative ways of defining "integration" that can provide valuable insights to the process of developing understanding across national boundaries?

Given a minimal commitment to settling conflicts by peaceful means in the North Atlantic community, Deutsch suggests other measures of integration. A second approach in determining the amount of cohesion is the amount of cooperation among states. The use of the transaction as an integrative indicator is emphasized in Deutsch's notion of "community," in which states must respond to each other's needs quickly and in a variety of ways (Deutsch et al., 1957, 44–53). The varied use of transactions in integrative studies can be seen in the use of goods exchanged or trade (Deutsch and Savage; Russett, 1965) or the number of daily airline flights between two countries (J. Galtung).

Russett argues that transactions can serve as a means of determining the "responsiveness" of states. This notion presumes that all members of a community have two characteristics. First, each subunit must have the capacity to act, which is dependent on wealth, natural resources and viable administrative agencies. This relates to the second element, which is frequent communication with other nations on a variety of indicators such as trade and tourism. All of the countries in the North Atlantic area would be ranked highly on both requisites especially when compared with nation-states in other areas (Russett, 1965, 26–33).[2]

However, transactions alone do not necessarily guarantee cohesion. Merritt's study (1964, 255–263) of England and the American colonies reveals that fairly high levels of transactional exchange between the colonies and their mother country did not preclude cleavage and ultimately division. In a more recent example, the United States and France have increased their relative magnitude of transactional exchange, but this disguises a series of policy disagreements over the last decade (Hoffman, 521–540).

As a result, integration theorists are attempting to find other aspects of community building which might be linked to interstate cooperation. A third approach is to focus on attitudes or perceptions of significant

---

2. In terms of absolute magnitudes, the smaller countries of the North Atlantic community such as Ireland and Luxembourg would not be ranked as highly, but relative indicators such as percentage of transactions exchanged within the area would keep all Western European countries ranked high (Brams, 1967).

groups within a nation, whether particular decision-makers or the public at large. Deutsch argues that critical links in the development of an integrated area are a positive affect directed toward other countries within the region and a desire to further efforts at achieving unification. Ultimately, regardless of how frequently transactions occur, popular beliefs hold the key to the development of a supranational community (Deutsch, 1957, 93). E. Haas (1958) argues that the views of important governmental decision-makers will determine the success of efforts at regional integration. This view is also adopted by Lindberg, who asserts that until the governmental elites of countries take a broader perspective in their approach to problem solving, integration cannot occur.

An intermediate position is adopted by Etzioni (1965, 4), who asserts that a focus on officials is not sufficient in delineating the likelihood of developing cohesion; he maintains that in addition to governmental leaders, that segment of the populace which is "politically aware" must also support integrative efforts.

In stressing the notion of "attitudinal integration," Deutsch asserts that mass opinion must be receptive in a variety of ways. First, other peoples must be viewed with positive affect. This is shown in a case study of a pluralistic security community involving the United States and West Germany in which attitudes of each toward the other are very supportive. In addition, there must be an element of concern above and beyond the national level. Mass opinion must be supportive of efforts at increasing cooperation between nations and must endorse such policies (Deutsch, 1959, 20–34). Such opinions are shown to exist in Western Europe in a recent study for certain selected countries (Deutsch et al., 1967, 265–275).[3]

However, in comparison with the number of transactional analyses in various geographical regions, there has been a dearth of investigations in the area of attitudinal integration (Klineberg; Snyder and Robinson). This is ironic given the importance placed on the pivotal role of public opinion in a study of conflict behavior throughout the world over many centuries (Wright). In addition, there have been few attempts to interrelate mass attitudes with other measures of integration such as transactions to determine the extent to which there is compatibility among the various indicators (Levi).

A fourth approach to the study of integration is one resembling the traditional focus of political science: the governmental institution. The focus shifts to the extent to which supranational institutions have wielded influence over the policies of member nation-states (Richardson). The

3. The countries involved were France, West Germany, Italy, and the Netherlands.

degree of autonomy granted to secretariat personnel is posited by E. Haas (1966) to be the key element leading to the success of collaboration in Western Europe. Lindberg documents the transformation of the Inner Six's secretariat from a passive stance of serving requests of member states to assumption of an active leadership role in determining policies to be adopted by the organization.[4] Etzioni (1965) argues that the Common Market Commission now has such a large discretionary role that "it has more power than the makers of the treaty envision" (233).

According to E. Haas (1958), the impetus of secretariat latitude in a supranational institution will lead to "spill-over" (5–16). Once an agreement is made to give a unit more authority, the likelihood that such agreements concerning the same items will be made in the future is increased. The institutional emphasis assumes that a series of agreements sponsored by the organization will multiply, leading to a commitment to peaceful relations. However, administrative spill-over is not yet sufficiently developed to guarantee peaceful relations among states (Wright).

The postulate that latitude among bureaucrats in supranational units indicates the most salient feature of collaboration is questionable. E. Haas (1966, 1–30) points to task expansion in the International Labor Organization, stressing a widening of tasks performed by officials; however, he is unable to specify how such latitude leads to a stronger commitment among member states to collaboration in the sphere of labor relations. Even Etzioni (1965, 229–284) argues that the Common Market's success could be traced to certain attitudes of key decision-makers and mass publics of participating nations.[5] As a result, most studies of integration focus on the perceptions of national publics or their leaders and interstate collaboration, instead of stressing policies of particular supranational organizations.[6]

Under the general rubric of integration, many empirical studies assess the magnitude of cohesion among various states. Efforts focus on the regional level (Deutsch, 1962) as well as the global level (E. Haas,

4. The counterpart of the Common Market is the European Free Trade Association, or Outer Seven, with the following members: Austria, Denmark, Great Britain, Norway, Portugal, Sweden, and Switzerland.
5. Etzioni (1965) asserts that the key aspect determining the extent to which collaboration will be achieved is the degree of identification with the larger community by the "politically aware" members of the state. This includes members of the government and those members of the mass public who are informed about international developments.
6. For example, Deutsch (1962) and Russett (1963) focus on behavior at the national level rather than supranational organizational consequences. Even E. Haas (1958) asserts that perceptions of national decision-makers are the determinants of policy latitude of bureaucrats in the Coal and Steel Community.

1961). Most research focuses on measures of cooperation and attitudes of governmental officials or national publics,[7] but little effort is made to examine the relationship between attitudes and indicators of mutual responsiveness such as transactions at the nongovernmental level and treaties within the governmental sphere. The problems of congruence among the indicators and the background variables alleged to predict to varying degrees of cehesion are examined in the next chapter.

A Model for the   How can the varied approaches to the study
Study of   of cohesion be interrelated into a model for
International   the study of international collaborative be-
Collaboration   havior? The following three-component model
    illustrates the framework that is derived from
the previous arguments.

Since nations are known to be selective with respect to whom they interact with, the model starts with the presumption that the basis of this selectivity can, in part, be explained by background characteristics and conditions.[8] Relevant background factors include properties of the geophysical environment, unit properties or attributes, and systemic properties. The first of these, geophysical properties, provide an indication of the material costs of intercourse between nations. The second set of variables refers to characteristics of the nations themselves and allows us to assess the mutual capabilities of two nations to act and interact. The third and final set of background variables is that of systemic properties. These serve to indicate past habits and memories of attention between nations as well as present capabilities arising from previous collaborative arrangements.

In linking background phenomena to interaction, the model assumes that the pattern of interaction between nations establishes their mutual relevance. The general hypothesis, then, is that the mutual behavioral relevance of two nations is, in part, a function of the various types of background factors associated with that nation-pair. Jacob and Teune

7. The terms *mass, national mass,* and *national publics* are all used to denote an opinion distribution of a sample of the total populace within (a) particular nation(s). This usage of terminology will also apply to ensuing chapters.

8. Although awkward, this observation might be more appropriately phrased as follows: The members of a nation are selective with respect to the nations with whose members they interact. Because it is unwieldy, we will not use this form of statement, even though it is technically in order. Thus, when we speak of nations interacting, we are not reifying the nations, but using the term "nation" as a convenient shorthand to denote the members of a group called a nation. When we speak of nations collaborating, on the other hand, we refer to arrangements between nations as corporate bodies acting through the agency of their respective governments.

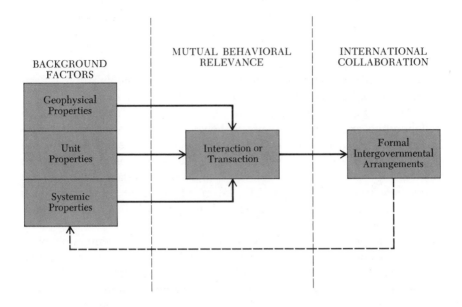

(23) identify three major types of interaction variables: *communication*—the interchange of messages, *trade*—the exchange of goods and services, and *mobility*—the movement of persons and/or frequency of personal contacts. Collectively, these are the variables that define the mutual relevance of two nations.

The second general proposition contained within the model is that mutual relevance established through the interactions and transactions between nations tend to lead to formalized collaborative arrangements between their governments. The model thus argues that formal inter-governmental collaboration is of a single genus and that the greater the mutual relevance the greater the number of collaborative arrangements. This is not to suggest that marginal changes in mutual relevance will necessarily have a uniform effect on the level or frequency of various types of substantive collaboration. Both the scope and level of collaboration may vary with the level of mutual relevance.

In addition to and following directly from the two general hypotheses discussed above, the model suggests that background phenomena are indirectly linked to formal collaboration between governments. This relationship is seen primarily as a result of the mutual relevance established by the patterns of relative interaction between two nations. In positing this intervening linkage, it is assumed that the various kinds of inter-nation interaction form a system of variables characterized by what general systems theorists term "equifinality" (McClelland, 1955, 30). However, the quantitative equivalence of these variables is not assumed. In other words, we assume that there are alternative ways of arriving at the same end. While one interactive channel may be more or less efficient than another in generating the need and desire for formal collaboration, it is the mutually reinforcing effect of a number of channels that is seen as the determining factor, rather than any one channel alone.

While the model tends to imply that formal intergovernmental collaboration arises as a response to behavioral patterns of mutual relevance, it is clearly possible for governments to attempt to promote mutual relevance through collaborative policies. This is to say that the relationship between mutual relevance and formal collaboration may be a two-way street. This is partially taken into account by the feedback loop in the model, although no formal attempt will be made to assess feedback, per se.

A final point needs to be made with respect to conception of internation collaboration. Since collaboration tends to imply cooperation, one might reasonably suppose that collaboration would fall somewhere in the upper half of a conflict-cooperation continuum running from, say, war to amalgamation. If this be so, we are clearly not looking at the full range of relevant behavior. Such a limitation could perhaps be justified by noting that substantial amount of recent research is devoted to the study of conflict behavior (Rummel, 1967; Singer and Small) or that the demand for manageability constrains the scope of the present inquiry. But perhaps no such apology is necessary.

There is ample reason to believe that conflict and cooperation are not unidemsional. Although far from conclusive, recent studies have indicated that international conflict and cooperation constitute independent behavioral dimensions (Rummel, 1966a; Rummel et al.). Intuitively, this observation may seem illogical; but it begins to make sense if one simply considers that the most violent individual conflicts often occur between friends and lovers (Coser, 60–65). Therefore, when we speak of collaboration, we envision not a continuum running from conflict to cooperation, but an isolation-collaboration continuum, à la Guetzkow (1957).

Conclusion   Drawing upon a number of dominant themes in the current international relations literature, we have outlined a simple model for the study of international collaborative behavior. Admittedly, the model does not do justice to the phenomenal complexity involved in the course of international affairs. But this is not its purpose. Its purpose is primarily heuristic, to abstract and simplify so as to allow us to zero in on a range of phenomena. The simplicity of the model will be vindicated insofar as it proves useful as an organizational scheme and a framework for analysis.

Our approach to the problem of international collaboration is distinctly ecological. We are not here concerned with the discrete behavior and attributes of individuals, per se, but rather with aggregate patterns of behavior and attributes which characterize nation-pairs.

The model we have outlined is predicated on two general propositions. Firstly, the mutual relevance of two nations—defined by the scope and intensity of their intercourse—is a function of the background properties associated with, and peculiar to, that nation-pair. Secondly, the greater the mutual relevance between two nations the greater the likelihood of more or less permanent, i.e., formal or institutional, cooperative arrangements arising between them. These general hypotheses are refined and made more specific in the next chapter.

The methodological implications of the model will be drawn out in detail in Chapter 4. For the moment, we may note that these implications are basically threefold: (1) the unit of analysis must be dyadic, i.e., one must consider nation-pairs;   (2) a number of variables must be considered simultaneously; while   (3) the identity or integrity of each variable must be preserved.

chapter 3

The Components
of Integration Theory

Introduction   In this chapter an effort is made to refine and elaborate the general notions presented in Chapter 2. A major portion of the chapter is devoted to identifying specific background variables of the three types—geophysical; unit, or societal; and systemic—and linking these variables to patterns of interaction between nations. These patterns of interaction are, in turn, linked to formal inter-governmental collaboration. Prior to addressing these two tasks, however, attention is directed to the interrelationships among the various types of interaction.

Mutual Relevance   We have argued that the mutual relevance *and the*   of two nations is established through the in-*Interrelation of*   tensity and extensity of interaction between *Interaction*   them. Since there are a multiplicity of chan-*Variables*   nels for international intercourse, no one channel is likely to be sufficient to indicate the mutual relevance of two nations. Rather, what is of more likely importance is the mutually reinforcing pattern of the multiplicity of the channels.

The need to focus on interactions beyond national boundaries is noted as a key to the development of cohesion between different states

(Guetzkow, 1950).[1] Meier defines such interaction as a transaction or "an exchange between countries that involves some communication of information and a transfer of people, goods or services" (40).

Russett (1963) argues that the hallmark of a supranational community is "responsiveness"; publics of various states must have available and use different means of communication to achieve collaboration. Deutsch (1960a, 147–155) finds that all successful security communities have a multiplicity of transaction channels performing a variety of common functions and purposes. Indeed, a high rate of transactional exchange within an area may mean that the community achieves a degree of integration (Deutsch, 1962, 212–218). E. Haas (1966) asserts that integration is "the process of increasing interaction so as to transcend national boundaries" (28).

This approach presumes that measuring the number of exchanges along with their magnitudes is the most important step in determining how people are connected with one another. The key is not in determining only which of the transactions such as trade or mail is the most important but in ascertaining the overall pattern of linkages between countries (Hoffman). Etzioni (1965, 43–64) argues that as the amount of goods and services across national boundaries increases, attempts at collaboration will increase.

Studies of transactional exchange exist for all major countries in the world (Brams, 1966), as well as for particular geographic areas (Deutsch, 1960a). A wide variety of exchanges ranging from tourism to diplomatic exchange have been examined in different studies (Angell; I. Galtung; Simon). Given the primacy of transactional exchange as an indicator of mutual salience, what are the findings concerning the linkage among these indicators?

Proposition 1—There is a strong interrelationship among various forms of transactional exchange.

Deutsch argues that responsiveness in terms of transactional exchange should be reinforcing. Countries having a relatively high amount of trade with one another should cooperate frequently in other areas such as tourism and student exchange. Similarly, countries which do not interact on one measure such as trade are not likely to reciprocate on others such as tourism (Deutsch, 1960a, 147–155).

Lipjhart studies two forms of transactions exchanged among eleven

---

1. Henceforth the term "transactional integration" will be used to refer to a high level of transactional exchange among nations on a variety of indicators. A "high level of exchange" means that at a minimum, the amounts exchanged on a particular item increase with the passage of time.

Western European countries on a dyadic basis.[2] In assessing trade and tourist patterns in 1956, Lipjhart finds those dyads having a relatively high level of trade are also likely to have high rates of tourism. Dyads involving the Scandinavian and the Benelux nations[3] are particularly noteworthy for their high level of transactional exchange attained on each measure. However, Lipjhart (260) is reluctant to generalize until other transactions are gathered and their interrelationships examined.

In a more limited study of twelve dyads involving four countries over a twenty-five-year span, Russett (1965, 37–46) posits a similar conclusion. France and West Germany show a high level of exchange on various indicators from mail to trade exchange;[4] similarly, dyads which have relatively little increase over time in amount of mail exchange are unlikely to have high rates of tourism or student exchange.[5] While all these examples provide evidence of a positive relationship among various interaction measures, in no case has this interrelationship been found great enough to suggest that any one variable is sufficient to serve as an indicator of all variables. In addition, the proposition concerning a high interrelationship among transactional indicators has yet to be tested at more than one point in time with a number of countries.

Interaction variables of all three of the types (viz., communications, trade, and mobility) identified by Jacob and Teune are used in this study. These will be discussed in detail in Chapter 4. For the moment we will simply offer a general proposition: various indicators of inter-nation interaction will tend to vary together.

Background Phenomena and Patterns of Mutual Relevance We are now prepared to link specific background factors with patterns of international intercourse. The framework employed arises directly from the model outlined in Chapter 2. Three types of background factors will be considered. Each type constitutes a set of predictors or independent variables which according to our model should help us understand and explain patterns of mutual behavioral relevance between nations. The

---

2. The countries are Austria, Belgium, Denmark, France, German Federal Republic, Great Britain, Italy, the Netherlands, Norway, Sweden, and Switzerland. A dyad refers to a nation-pair such as the United States–Great Britain. The formula to determine how many dyads are included is $N(N-1)$, or 110 pairs for Lipjhart's sample.
3. The Scandinavian countries included are Denmark, Norway and Sweden; the Benelux countries are Belgium, Luxembourg, and the Netherlands.
4. Prior to World War II, the figures refer to all of Germany; since 1945 the figures are limited to the German Federal Republic.
5. An example of a dyad where this pattern emerged is France–Germany.

first set of predictors concerns properties of the geophysical environment. The second are societal, or unit, properties; the third, systemic properties. The criteria or dependent variables in each case are measures of the scope and intensity of inter-nation interaction.

Geophysical As we have previously noted, transnational
Properties intercourse involves costs for the nations involved. In material terms, these costs are presumably a function of the physical barriers separating two nations. In general, the physical obstacles to intercourse should be less with geographic proximity.

GEOGRAPHICAL PROXIMITY

Consistent with the cost argument, geographical distance is frequently assumed to be an important factor facilitating or impeding internation interaction. The assumption is generally based on something like the "principle of least effort" postulated by Zipf (1949).

Proposition 2a—The more geographically proximate two nations, the more they will tend to interact with each other.

A number of scholars give particular emphasis to the importance of territorial contiguity. Clearly, the ease of transportation and communications afforded two nations by a common boundary favors the development of more intense patterns of interaction. Contiguity is thus often cited as a central factor in the growth of international regionalism.

Propinquity also has relevance to the salience of certain key attitudinal clusters. If we define "mutual relevance" to include favorable mass predispositions toward other nations, geographical proximity is postulated to be of prime importance. In a study of nine nations in the late 1940's,[6] Buchanan and Cantril argue that the extent to which national masses perceive other nations favorably is a key ingredient to achieving world peace. Geographical proximity would determine the extent to which people would view other nations with positive affect. Proximate nations such as West Germany and France would be more likely to have reciprocal positive affect than would nations separated by an ocean such as the United States and France. A common boundary affords a maximum opportunity to learn about the attitudes and values of other nations (Buchanan and Cantril, 38–44).

6. The nine nations were Australia, France, Great Britain, Italy, the Netherlands, Norway, Mexico, the United States, and West Germany.

Support for the importance of geographical proximity also emerges from a study by Brams (1967, 1–18). He divides the world into six geographical regions[7] and studies trade patterns within and between regions. He finds proximity to be the most important predictor of trade flows, as countries in Western Europe concentrate trade activities in that area rather than with other regions.

Other studies reach similar conclusions. Linnemann finds geographical distance to be an important factor in predicting international trade. Lipjhart concludes that proximity is closely related to tourism and trade in Western Europe.

Often the importance of proximity is mitigated by recognition of other factors, particularly modern technology. In fact, Jacob and Teune (18) suggest that owing to these factors, the direct influence of geographical distance may be negligible. One may wonder, however, if the influence of geography or international rations, whatever it may be, has been substantially altered by factors such as technology. Deutsch (1957) finds that despite rapid transportation, mass communications, and literacy, modern life does not tend "to be more international than life in past decades or centuries, and hence [no] more conducive to the growth of international or supranational institutions" (23).

Proposition 2b—Geographical proximity does not significantly influence the relative intercourse between two nations.

Proposition 2c—The more geographically remote two nations the more they will tend to interact with each other.

All evidence does not indicate a close linkage between proximity and collaboration in terms of cooperative attitudes and high levels of interaction. Some such as Jacob and Teune (16–18) dispute its alleged primacy by noting strong affective and transactional ties between countries which are not proximate such as in the British Commonwealth. In direct juxtaposition to the dominant presumption regarding the influence of physical proximity, Liska (1962, 13) and Wolfers (209) argue that geographical distance may play an ameliorative role in the relations of nations. Basically, their arguments suggest that in order to safeguard its integrity and freedom of action and to avoid obvious dependency ties, a nation may seek to avoid intense relations with more proximate nations. Relationships with more remote nations then command greater attention and interaction.

Several empirical studies denigrate the alleged primacy of proxim-

---

7. The six areas are America, Asia, Africa, Western Europe, Eastern Europe, and the Middle East.

ity in predicting types of ensuing interstate relationships. Provisional findings reported by Deutsch (1960b) show proximity has only limited effects on the distribution of world trade. Merritt (1964, 262–263) in a study specifically designed to explore Zipf's hypothesis in the context of American-British relations is able to find only mixed results and concludes that the influence of geographical distance, per se, has been greatly exaggerated by Zipf.

The conclusions that can be drawn from all of this are uncertain. The Merritt study is restricted in scope, as he was dealing with only one nation-pair. Lipjhart feels the conclusions so obvious that he considers it unnecessary to subject them to a formal test. His referent perspective, however, is unclear. We would certainly expect that the more restricted one's perspective in terms of area considered, the less pronounced the effect of geographical proximity.

Despite the influence attributed to proximity one way or the other, its effect on the relations between nations has been the subject of relatively little empirical research. Typically, one or two specific cases are offered either to support or refute the general hypothesis that proximity significantly affects inter-nation intercourse. More rigorous empirical research is needed since the alleged linkage remains an open question.

Unit Properties   The second type of background factors to be considered is the set of unit properties, characteristics of nation-pairs arising from the internal, or societal, characteristics of the two units involved. We might recall that these properties are seen primarily as determinants of the mutual capacity of two nations to act and interact. Insofar as material capabilities are involved, we are interested both in the level of capability present in a nation-pair and commonality of that capability. While the former presumably indicates the capacity for action, the latter is assumed to foster the sort of mutuality of knowledge, interests, and identifications necessary for responsive interaction. With respect to variables indicative of cultural values and historical experience, we are, likewise, interested in the extent to which these are shared by the members of a nation-pair.

(1a) BELIEF SYSTEMS AND SYSTEM PRACTICES: HOMOGENEITY OF MAJOR POLITICAL VALUES

Students of international community have almost universally stressed the importance of mutually compatible internal political attitudes, values, and practices as a factor in the establishment of inter-nation bonds.

Proposition 3a—The more homogeneous the major political values and institutions of two nations, the more they will tend to interact with each other.

Deutsch and his collaborators (1957) in their seminal study of the North Atlantic area conclude that such value compatibility is, in fact, essential to the establishment of the enduring and mutually rewarding relationships between nations which characterize what they term a "security-community." In reporting their findings they state,

> Values were most effective politically when they were not held merely in abstract terms, but when they were incorporated in political institutions and in habits of political behavior which permitted these values to be acted on in such a way as to strengthen people's attachment to them. This connection between values, institutions, and habits we call a "way of life," and it turned out to be crucial [47].

According to Jacob and Teune, this means that "countries with democratic political institutions are likely to develop an attachment to these institutions and that this then tends to produce a favorable attitude toward other democracies. . . . The same argument would hold for communist nations" (37–38).

Consonant with the above, Lindgren tells us that the close ties between Norway and Sweden arose and are sustained, in part, from "the possession of similar sets of political values and a willingness to act together on political problems in ways commensurate with these values" (281). Similarly, Russett (1963) stresses the importance of value homogeneity and institutions in American–British relations. E. Haas (1961) points to the same thing with respect to the relations among Western European states generally.

Proposition 3b—The degree of homogeneity of political values will not significantly effect the level of relatve interaction between two nations.

To counterpoise the above observations, Etzioni (1965) notes that relatively strong relational ties may exist in the face of marked political heterogeneity. As examples, he points out that "NATO includes both firmly established democracies and Portugal. Democratic Costa Rica and authoritarian Nicaragua share the bonds of the Central American Common Market" (24).

Shared political values seemingly would tend to foster the sort of mutual identifications, knowledge, and functional interests conducive to interaction. But, on the other hand, unless a nation's political values and institutions are tuned to its traditions and internal needs, they may be destructive to its capacity to interact externally with other nations regardless of the political values involved. Thus, rationales can be found to support both conflicting hypotheses.

(1b) BELIEF SYSTEMS AND SYSTEM PRACTICES: THE SALIENCE OF CERTAIN KEY ATTITUDES

Another approach to studying the problem of values or beliefs of a particular nation is to focus on certain mass perceptions which are generally held throughout a particular national populace.[8] In evaluating different approaches to the study of community formation, Deutsch and his associates (1957) assert that a prerequisite of interstate interaction is a "sense of community" created among the populace. Unless certain attitudes are accepted by the public, cohesion in any lasting sense is not feasible. They also assert that this perspective includes "a matter of mutual sympathies and loyalties, a we-feeling, a sense of trust and mutual consideration. Peaceful change could not be achieved without this kind of relationship" (36). Their research indicates that nearly all collaborative efforts in Western Europe over the last two centuries have mass support in participating nations.[9]

The importance of the attitudinal component of integration is demonstrated by Jacob and Teune (1964), who review all approaches and conclude that the following definition is the most appropriate: "Political integration is a state of mind to be cohesive, to act together, to be committed to mutual programs" (10). In a separate piece on the likelihood of future collaborative attempts, Levi (111–126) posits the amount of acceptance by the mass population of the participating nations as crucial in determining the success of unification efforts.

Given the importance of the attitudinal element, there are three key issues around which most research has been grouped: (1) the extent to which different attitudinal components are interrelated; (2) the stability of attitudes over time, and (3) the responsiveness of attitudes to the creation of supranational structures.

---

8. Mass attitudes are treated primarily as background properties (predictor variables), but are occasionally treated as aspects of mutual salience (criterion variables) to examine the feedback or the impact of other variables on attitude orientations.
9. The focus on mass opinion does not denigrate the importance of the opinions of governmental decision-makers. However, given the alleged salience of mass opinion in achieving cohesion and the dearth of studies on the topic a focus on mass attitudes can be justified. Numerous elite studies have been completed (E. Haas, 1958; Lindberg; Deutsch et al., 1957).

THE INTERRELATIONSHIP OF ATTITUDINAL COMPONENTS OF INTEGRA-
TION The investigator must take care to be explicit about what types
of mass views on foreign policy issues are relevant to attitudinal integration. Deutsch (1957, 36) posits two aspects of mass opinion which reflect
popular commitment to collaboration; first is the matter of "mutual
sympathies and loyalties." In this instance, the focus is on mass perceptions of other nations, with positive affect being a requisite for a sense of
community.

Scott (1965, 72–74) asserts that there is a basic tendency in most
nations for publics to "like" or "dislike" other foreign countries. Queener
also argues that one key aspect in the development of internationalist
attitudes is the "affective component," as people must perceive other
nations as "friendly" prior to creating a world community.

A second element of attitudinal integration[10] refers to support of
cooperative actions in accordance with outlooks toward individual countries. Deutsch and his colleagues (1967, 36) asserts that not only must
masses view other nations favorably but policies supporting regional
unification must also have popular endorsement; for example, national
publics in Western Europe must view other nations as friendly, but must
also endorse efforts at achieving further unity such as expansion of the
Common Market.

Queener refers to this aspect of mass opinion as the "action component," which is the second requisite to the development of a political
community based on similar beliefs. Any movement toward international
collaboration, he feels, must have a basis of popular support, since governments ultimately reflect popular wishes. Scott (1965) also identifies the
same two aspects of opinion as the keys in determining the content of "an
international image" which influences the extent of intergovernmental
cooperation.[11]

The action component is also a critical element in Etzioni's definition of integration; commitment to a community in terms of supporting
its policies such as a single Common Market encompassing all of the
North Atlantic area countries would be needed. He speculates that the
idea of a united Europe is not yet broadly based. However, he notes

10. Henceforth the term "attitudinal integration" will refer to two types of attitudes:
the affective component and the action, or policy, component.
11. Scott finds that nations in which masses have a favorable perception of populaces
in other countries are more likely to be collaborative than nation-pairs without a
bond of positive affect. He also posits a third component concerned with the extent
to which nations are "threatened" by an external power, particularly the Soviet Union.
Notions concerning war expectancy have been explored in various surroundings
(Deutsch et al., 1967; Scott, 1965).

some progress, as the popular support for a supranational base has gained wider adherence among the national publics of Western Europe (Etzioni, 1965).

Proposition 4a—The affective component of attitudinal integration is highly correlated with an action component of attitudinal integration.

Given these two separate components of mass attitudes, what about their interrelationship? There is some evidence to indicate a close linkage. Scott (1965, 74–77) argues that there was an attitudinal hierarchy in mass opinions. People who are favorably disposed toward other nations are likely to favor policies promoting regional integration. He relies primarily on an analysis of Canadian poll data over time, in which those who were positive in their perceptions of Germany, Italy, and Japan were more likely to favor increased trade with all nations.

Scott's findings are also supported by case studies of various North Atlantic nations. In a study of the British "elite" (i.e., those with a college education), positive attitudes toward the United States are closely linked with expansion of the Common Market and strengthening of the military alliance network in Western Europe (Abrams, 236–246). In a study of West German mass attitudes, positive evaluation of France is related to expansion of the European Coal and Steel Community and the development of a United States of Europe (Kriesberg, 28–42). This linkage is also endorsed by Russett (1965, 46–54), who finds that the negative perception of other nations by the French is linked to strong opposition to the existing alliance structure.[12] In an American study relating perceptions of objects to policies associated with those perceptions, there is a strain toward attitudinal consistency in that people endorsed policies congruent with their outlooks; consistency also increases with knowledge and educational attainment (Gamson and Modigliani, 187–199).

Proposition 4b—The affective component of attitudinal integration is not highly correlated with an action component of attitudinal integration.

However, all evidence does not indicate that both measures of attitudinal integration are highly interrelated. Deutsch and Edinger (21–22, 215) argue that affective orientations are not that closely linked with policy preferences.[13] In analyzing German opinion during the mid-1950s, they found there was a favorable German perception of the United States

12. The countries involved were Italy, Great Britain, and West Germany.
13. Deutsch's measures of affective perceptions revolve around the extent to which the two countries had good feelings about the other (i.e., United States and West Germany).

and Great Britain;[14] however, the German public did not view favorably efforts at achieving a greater amount of regional unification such as the Paris agreements and treaties concerning the European Defense Community.

Beloff (56–73) argues that the principal reason behind the slow pace at which interstate collaboration has been proceeding concerns the discrepancy between the affective and the action components. He speculates that there was a general reciprocal positive affect between Great Britain and other countries in Western Europe, but that there is little popular support for developing supranational institutions. He asserts that governmental slowness was merely a reflection of a lack of mass consensus for collaboration.

The two conflicting strains are based on a series of case studies or speculative interpretation. Whether there is the relationship between these two separate attitudinal components posited by Deutsch remains to be investigated. Given these two components of attitudinal integration, what can be posited about their stability?

THE STABILITY OF ATTITUDINAL COMPONENTS OF UNIT PROPERTIES   A key notion in the development of a sense of community is the extent to which mass attitudes are stable and reflective of some underlying sentiment or are subject to great changes in short time-intervals.[15]

Proposition 5a—Mass opinion is "moody," or unstable, with respect to both the affective and action components.

In one of the first attempts to systematically analyze the trends in attitudes over time,[16] Almond focuses on American attitudes toward Western European countries and international organizations such as the United Nations. The principal finding is the inherent instability of mass attitudes. In examining public responses to a variety of foreign policy questions between 1945–1950,[17] Almond finds noticeable shifts over short periods of time for no apparent reason.[18] Consequently, he concludes that masses are "moody" and that little importance can be attached to their feelings. Almond (54–55) also links his substantive findings to earlier

14. Eighty percent of the German people viewed the United States in a favorable perspective in the mid-1950's, while about 60 percent had positive perceptions of Great Britain.
15. All literature reviewed on mass opinion refers only to the realm of foreign policy concerns unless otherwise noted.
16. "Stability" in this discussion is defined as a persistent percentage breakdown to a question asked at different intervals of time.
17. Questions asked referred to perceptions of the Soviet Union, the United Nations, likelihood of war in the next decade, trustworthiness of allies, etc.
18. Opinion shifts of 20–30 percent occurred within a few months on several issues such as satisfaction with the United Nations.

speculative works such as Lowell's treatise (7–30) on the link between mass sentiments and conflict and concludes that change is the hallmark of opinion and the spirit of our time is ephemeral.

Almond (92–99) notes a possible danger: given the ephemeral nature of opinion on foreign policy issues, people might overreact to changes in the contemporary political scene, thereby forcing policy-makers into untenable positions in determining policies. He argues that only if there is some stability in attitudes can governments effectively pursue policies of collaboration.

Another empirical study which supports Almond's findings concerns American attitudes toward the United Nations over a ten-year period, from 1945 to 1955. Moodiness is present in the mass appraisal of the organization's activities with support running from 26 percent to 66 percent within a time interval of less than five years. However, dissatisfaction with the organization was stable until the United Nations intervened in the Korean conflict. Since this action supported the United States position, a more positive perception of the organization's work among the American public is not too surprising (Scott and Withey, 40–50).

In reviewing public opinion studies in various nations, Kelman concludes that mass opinion on policy issues and perceptions of others is marked by a lack of structure and stability. However, he is primarily interested in the amount of information possessed by mass publics on various foreign affairs' issues. Given a criterion which requires a high amount of information and awareness, Kelman's support (580–581) of the absence of widespread mass awareness is not surprising.

Proposition 5b—Mass opinion is stable with respect to both affective and action components.

Given this strain in opinion research, all evidence does not support the notion of opinion instability. A study of American foreign policy attitudes a decade after Almond's investigation challenges the notion of moodiness. Key attempts to ascertain the nature of the alleged volatility, but finds American attitudes to be consistent in percentage distributions over a span of several years. In examining the same questions repeated over a series of years,[19] Key concludes that the decade of the 1950's reflected a high degree of stability. He asserts that attitudes toward other nations may vary from nation to nation, but these outlooks have a high degree of stability; the oversensitivity to events discussed by Almond was overplayed as sentiments are enduring and not subject to radical change. Key (256–257) would not argue that the American public be-

19. Questions dealt with the friendliness of enemies such as the Soviet Union, with American allies, likelihood of war, etc.

trayed any substantive sophistication on complex foreign policy questions, but that on issues of perceptions of the friendliness of other countries and policies supporting collaboration, stability rather than moodiness is the norm.

In an attempt to determine the generalizability of Almond's notions in other countries, Deutsch and Edinger (21–22) studied German foreign policy attitudes over a decade; in the interval between 1947–1957, mass opinions varied little in perceptions of the United States and Great Britain. The lack of volatility is shown more recently in an examination of opinion data in the 1960's with supportive Western European attitudes toward unity and only minor alternations in the past decade in France, West Germany, Italy, and Great Britain (Deutsch et al., 1967, 245–251).

In an elaborate study of several nations in different time-periods, an effort is made to assess the impact of such well-known events as the Hungarian revolt and the abortive American invasion of Cuba in 1961 to predict opinion change.[20] In most instances, little change is found in mass attitudes, and the authors argue that mass opinion is not as vulnerable to major occurrences as might be imagined (Deutsch and Merritt, 135–137).

There appear to be two separate strains in studies dealing with the amount of stability in mass attitudes which require further investigation. Almond and others argue that opinion is superficial, moody, and vulnerable to overreaction to certain occurrences or events. However, others argue that opinion patterns are not nearly as susceptible to rapid change as earlier suspected. There are possible answers for this lack of congruence. In the late 40's and early 50's, the Soviet threat was very proximate in the lives of those in the North Atlantic area, and opinion was responsive to various actions made by major powers such as entry into the Korean War. In the ensuing decade, the threat has been mitigated and Almond could agree that greater stability could emerge (Spanier). Secondly, in some areas, opinion may be more stable than others. Key finds that opinions regarding perceptions of other nations are more stable than distributions on questions dealing with war expectancy.

In specifying the stability of integrative attitudes, the key consideration is specification of the types of opinions essential for ensuing collaborative efforts such as the affective and action components. Another consideration is the extent to which measures of attitudinal integration will become more positive with the creation of organizational machinery transcending national boundaries.

THE INTERRELATIONSHIP BETWEEN INDICATORS OF ATTITUDINAL ORIENTATION AND INTERACTION   Given the two separate indicators of attitudes

20. The countries involved include France, West Germany, Great Britain, Italy, and the United States.

and transactional exchange measures, Deutsch and his colleagues (1957, 46–65) assert that their congruence is essential to the development of a supranational political community. To achieve an ultimate state of unification, they find that nations must cooperate with one another and national publics must perceive other nations favorably and support policies favoring cohesion; whenever all these components are not present, efforts at amalgamating political units fragment.

> **Proposition 6a—High levels of transactional exchange will be highly correlated with the affective and policy components of mass opinion.**

In a study of community formation in the North Atlantic area, Deutsch (1962) asserts that mass attitudes and transactions are linked. His findings indicate that active popular support has not been crucial in the early stage of unifications movements in various case studies over the last two centuries;[21] mass support comes only at a later stage after states develop many forms of collaboration, from trade to intergovernmental agreements in the signing of treaties.

Inglehart (1967, 91–105) also supports the convergence of attitudes and transactions in the North Atlantic area; in using mass endorsement of expanding cooperation and trade patterns, he finds that attitudinal and transactional integration are increasing and will not peak until 1975, although he does not assert that one preceded the other. Congruence is found in small groups research where friendship and interaction are interrelated (Homans).

Of particular importance is the type of exchange which involves personal contact such as tourism. Reigrotski and Anderson (515–528) find that when Germans travel to France periodically, their favorable perceptions of the other country are more likely to emerge; and positive affect is more likely as the frequency of trips increases. A link between travel and attribution of positive affect is also shown in a study comparing French businessmen who traveled to other nations with those who did not leave France. Merchants venturing to other nations were more likely to have pro-European attitudes and were less protectionist in domestic trade policies (Lerner, 212–221.)

Student exchange can also lead to the development of more friendly attitudes. I. Galtung (258–275) finds that such interaction leads to shared

---

21. Examples of the case studies investigated include the union of the American colonies in 1789; German unification in 1871; the union of Norway and Sweden in 1814 leading to the dissolution in 1905; the creation of the Hapsburg Empire and its collapse in 1918; and the creation and destruction of the Union of Great Britain and Ireland in the early 1900s. For these and other case studies, see Deutsch et al. (1957).

values, as exchange students are more likely to favor policies increasing cooperation with other nations when returning to their home country than students who have not matriculated in schools of another country.

Proposition 6b—High levels of transactional exchange will not be highly correlated with the affective and policy components.

However, the evidence suggesting a close linkage between the two sets of indicators of integration is not completely supportive. In a recent study, Deutsch (1967) modifies many of his earlier assertions. Focusing primarily on France and West Germany, he finds that the attitudinal components of integration are present with mass perceptions of each other revealing more positive affect with the passage of time. In addition, there is an increase in the importance of the viewpoint of a united Europe in both countries particularly from the late 1950's. He asserts that the acceptance of the notion of Atlantic unity is fairly widespread among all groups in the two countries.

Yet the picture presented concerning attempts to achieve cohesion in Western Europe is fairly pessimistic. This is due primarily to the trend appearing in measures of transactional exchange over the last decade. There is no similar increase in the level of transactional exchange as with attitudinal indicators. Using an index of Relative Acceptance (RA index),[22] Deutsch, et al. (1967) examines trade patterns in the Atlantic area over the past seventy years. He finds a peak reached in 1948, which he attributes to the American effort to rebuild Western Europe, but since then the relative acceptance scores for trade and mail have been much lower.[23]

Deutsch and his associates (1967, 218–239) then examine other kinds of transaction flows (tourism, student exchange) and find that a peak occurred around 1958, a decade later than the apex reached in trade. Since that time there has been no appreciable increase in the level of transactional exchange; the same pattern is found in content analysis of newspaper editorials in France and West Germany for frequency of use of collaborative symbols.

In a similar study, Merritt (1966) looks at relations among the American colonies in the forty-year period prior to independence. Relying

22. The RA index measures how many more or fewer percent two countries interact with one another than would be expected by random probability and total volume of exchange on a particular indicator. As a score increases over time, the level of exchange between two countries is increasing. Applications of this method can be seen in studies by Brams (1966), Lipjhart, and Deutsch and Savage (1960).
23. In 1948, the RA score for those countries now members of the Common Market was 1.07. By 1963 the RA score for the same countries on trade was .77. A high RA score indicates a more cohesive unit.

primarily on content analysis of newspapers for occurrence of collaborative themes, he reports that a temporary peak in the use of integrative
symbols was reached akin to 1948 or 1958, then a temporary decline
resembling the last decade, and finally a rise to an even higher level—
all in the course of a few decades. However, Deutsch (1962, 212–218)
foresees no such trend in the Atlantic area in the ensuing decade; he
asserts that European politics will be focused on the problems of nation-
states, not on efforts at developing further unification or on supranational
institutions.

An alternative interpretation of the data has been presented by
Inglehart (1967, 100–105), who asserts that in terms of absolute numbers
and rate of increase, the amount of exchange on various transactional
indicators has risen steadily in the last decade; the only indicator which
has slowed in rate of increase is tourism, but this might only reflect the
reaching of a saturation point on that particular indicator. Inglehart also
argues that the level of integration demanded by Deutsch is unrealistic
and that any comparison of present-day Atlantic transactions with those
in 1948 can be misleading because of the artificial structuring by a great
amount of American aid and relocation following the war.[24]

Another point in dispute, other than the convergence of attitudinal
and transactional measures of integration, is the likelihood that differing
kinds of interactions will have attitudinal consequences. A study of the
effects of foreign travel on American businessmen indicates that travel
does not have a pervasive impact. Travel does not make businessmen
more supportive of policies favoring regional unification, but merely
broadens their range of problem awareness (Pool, Keller, and Bauer,
172–175).

A second aspect of the interrelationship of attitudes and transactions is that of dyad convergence.

Proposition 7a—High levels of transactional exchange lead to equivalent dyadic mass perceptions in attributions of positve affect toward the other.

In small group studies, Scott (1965, 94) asserts that increased interaction between individuals leads to greater dyadic congruence in reciprocal perceptions. On the level of national publics, Etzioni (1965, 255–
257) asserts that an increase in cooperation between nations leads to congruence in reciprocal perceptions of masses. In Western Europe during
the early 1950's, he finds that an increase in transactional exchange led

24. One of the problems with the RA index alluded to by Inglehart is that only one
variable (e.g., trade) can be considered at a time. While those using the RA index
such as Deutsch could examine trade patterns at various points in time, relationships
among several measures, such as trade, mail, and tourism, cannot be investigated
with this technique.

to more favorable perceptions of efforts to transcend national boundaries with national masses perceiving other nations in Western Europe with more positive affect.

Propostion 7b—High levels of transactional exchange do not lead to equivalent dyadic mass perceptions in attributions of positive affect toward the other.

The principal study disputing the notion of dyadic equivalence concerns the American colonies and England prior to 1776. Prior to the Revolutionary War, transactional exchange between the colonies and England reached its highest peak, and the English were favorable in their outlook toward the colonies. However, popular attitudes toward Britain were not favorable and the union finally crumbled, even with interaction on a variety of measures (Merritt, 1966).

(2) CULTURAL HOMOGENEITY

Cultural similarity is also often deemed to be an important element in the development of amiable cooperative bonds between nations.

Proposition 8a—The more culturally homogeneous two nations the more they will tend to interact with each other.

Guetzkow (1957) phrases the hypothesis thus, "The greater the similarity of language, customs and ideology among nations, the more easily will their members collaborate with one another" (57). Certainly, the ease of communications and common problem-solving orientations arising from shared cultural traditions would intuitively seem a boon to inter-nation intercourse.

Considerable evidence has been offered in support of the hypothesis. In his study of Norway and Sweden, Lindgren concludes that language and religious similarities, although not sufficient to support amalgamation, serves to gird the cooperative bonds between these two nations. Similarly, Russett finds cultural homogeneity to be an asset to American-British relations (1963) and to inter-nation collaboration in the North Atlantic region generally (1965). Buchanan and Cantril find common cultural traditions and common language in particular to be positively associated with mutually friendly perceptions and attitudes between nations. Tentative findings described by Deutsch (1960b) also suggest a strong correlation between trade and language and cultural homogeneity. Additional support for the hypothesis is provided by Lipjhart who demonstrated a positive correlation between cultural homogeneity and tourism in Western Europe. Further congruence is provided by Emerson and Burton, who note the cultural moorings of Pan-Africanism and the Pan-African union. According to them, one of the basic elements of this movement is the concept of "Negritude," which bases itself explicitly on the notion of the "Negro race."

Proposition 8b—Cultural homogeneity will not significantly influence the pattern of interaction between two nations.

However, not all research supports the link between homogeneity and intercourse. Compelling as the arguments and evidence supporting propositions may be, there has, nonetheless, been dissent. For example, Morgenthau argues that cultural similarity is largely irrelevant in the relations of nations. He contends that the "sharing of the same intellectual and esthetic experiences by members of different nations does not create a society, for it does not create morally and politically relevant actions on the part of the members of different nations with respect to each other which they would not have undertaken had they not shared in those experiences" (522). To buttress his arguments, he points out that

> the wars among the Greek city-states, the European wars of the Middle Ages, the Italian wars of the Renaissance, the religious wars of the sixteenth and seventeenth centuries, even the wars of the eighteenth century, insofar as the elite was concerned, were fought within the framework of a homogeneous culture. These cultures had all essentials in common: language, religion, education, literature, art. Yet these cultures did not create a community, coextensive with themselves, that could have kept disruptive tendencies in check and channeled them into peaceful outlets [522].

Etzioni (1965) also voices reservation about the attribution of an important ameliorating influence to cultural homogeneity. While granting that it may have some influence, he shows that for almost every case supporting the cultural homogeneity hypothesis, a counterexample can be found to refute it.

(3a) COMMON HISTORICAL EXPERIENCE: INTERNAL FACTORS

Common historical experience is yet another potential source of common identifications, knowledge, and mutual predictability that might facilitate intercourse between states. The historic variables we have in mind include the relative age of two countries, sovereignty-dependency relations, historical stability, and wartime alignments.

Proposition 9a—The more similar two nations in terms of their historical experience, the more they will tend to interact with each other.

Povolny notes the cohesive influence of a common colonial fate, but cautions against attributing too much influence to it (306). Consistent with this, Organski argues that the historic relations among colonial powers are quite distinct from those among noncolonizing and newly independent nations. Following and elaborating on this theme, both Emerson and Burton contend that anticolonialism and a sense of mutuality of interest in freedom provide a basis for close relational bonds between newer states. Organski observes, however, that old dependency ties may linger and, for that matter, provide the basis for new relational ties as in the case of the British Commonwealth. Deutsch (1960b) finds indications of this phenomenon in the analysis of trade flows.

(3b) COMMON HISTORICAL EXPERIENCE: WARTIME ALIGNMENTS

A particularly salient aspect of historical experience is previous alignment during a war. For example, to what extent is collaboration during the 1950's a consequence of friendships and animosities generated by the Second World War? This question has particular relevance to the North Atlantic area since most of the region's members were key wartime protagonists. Buchanan and Cantril argue that alliance patterns are capable of predicting which dyads have reciprocal positive affect in the succeeding years. Strong positive affect existed after the war between the publics of the wartime Allies: the United States, France, and Great Britain. Recently, these close perceptual ties have decayed (Merritt and Puchala). Hoffman (1963, 521–544) asserts that the sense of community and mutual relevance is stronger in the North Atlantic area because of a common wartime experience; the passage of time has not eliminated the memory of a global conflict as an important determinant of attitudinal integration and the propensity to interact with one another.

Proposition 9b—General commonality of historical experience will be largely irrelevant to the patterns of interaction between nations.

There is a lack of complete congruence among those speculating on the primacy of history and its eventual impact on interstate relations. Burton, as well as Liska, asserts that one historical component, stability, is not clearly linked to collaboration. Nations with a past of domestic instability often attempt to establish relations with more stable nations to promote internal stability. Historic stability might be indicative of the ability to go it alone, as it is a basis for inter-nation collaboration (Deutsch, 1954).

With respect to the problem of wartime alignments and eventual consequences, the pattern is similarly confused. A notable exception is the dyad of France–West Germany, where transactional exchanges have increased at a rapid rate and each public views the other with positive affect (Deutsch et al., 1967, 218–239). In addition, wartime allies can drift apart. World War II appears to have had a detrimental impact on Anglo-American relations, as there has been stagnation in transactional exchange and attributions of positive affect; and postwartime alliances have been unable to recement the relationship (Russett, 1963, 196–207). The general findings for a larger number of dyads in Western Europe in terms of wartime impact have yet to be determined.

In summary, there is an absence of clarity as to whether or not historical experience in a variety of forms has any significant impact on patterns of inter-nation relations. On the face of the problem, plausible arguments can be made both for and against the importance of a general commonality of historical experience as an element affecting the patterns of collaboration.

(4) SOCIAL WELFARE VALUES AND THEIR LEVEL OF REALIZATION

Homogeneity in terms of social welfare values is still another possible basis for mutual identifications and shared functional interests. The extent to which these values are realized in two nations also should relate to their capacities for mutual responsiveness (Deutsch, 1961).

> **Proposition 10a**—The greater the homogeneity of two nations with respect to social welfare, the more those two nations will tend to interact.

> **Proposition 10b**—The greater the average level of welfare achievement in two nations, the more those two nations will tend to interact.

Lindgren reports that the common desire to maintain a high level of social welfare has been a factor promoting the intense amiable relations that exist between Norway and Sweden. Many observers today regard the growing homogeneity of the United States and the Soviet Union in terms of social welfare values and their realization as a major contributing factor in the tenuous but hopeful movement toward an East-West détente. In contrast, one of the factors that seems to have undermined the Federation of the West Indies is the high level of disparity in social welfare expenditures among the member islands (Etzioni, 1965).

Both common social values and comparable levels of welfare achievement would seemingly tend to blend into and become a part of that complex of variables which is called a distinctive way of life. There is ample evidence to suppose that homogeneity and the level of social welfare would contribute to the intensity of mutual relevance.

Proposition 10c—Neither homogeneity of social welfare nor the level of welfare achievement will significantly affect the pattern of interaction between two nations.

One must note, however, that many nations with high levels of social welfare seek to promote the same values in countries most distinguished from them in these terms. Such efforts are abetted by the fact that there seems to exist near-universal agreement on the values of health, education, and employment. The distinction appears to hinge primarily on the level of achievement of these values. The efforts of the more affluent to uplift "less-fortunate" nations, coupled with the welfare aspirations of the latter, suggest that the level of social welfare and degree of homogeneity between two nations in these terms may be of little relevance to the intensity of the patterns of interaction between them.

(5) INTERNAL SOCIOECONOMIC DEVELOPMENT

Observations regarding the prospects for supranational collaboration and international cooperation tend to be much more sanguine with respect to developed nations than underdeveloped ones (Davis; Gordon; E. Haas, 1961).

Proposition 11a—The greater the average level of internal development, the more two nations will tend to interact.

Assessments of the relationship are generally based on the presumed dynamics of development itself. In the words of Schokking and Anderson,

> For decades industrialism has been revising the workways and consuming habits of people everywhere. It has enabled cities to grow and the urban way of life to spread. Urbanization is the great outreaching dynamic, breaking down isolation and encroaching upon tradition. It demands access and stimulates mobility. As earlier it resisted being confined to city walls, now it resists being confined to limited political areas [409].

In a more elaborate analysis, Etzioni (1965) has identified three possible reasons for higher levels of interaction and collaboration among more developed nations. First, in an argument similar to Schokking and Anderson's, Etzioni points out "the association between the level of education of citizens and the extent of their horizon of information and identification" (319). Clearly, the high level of illiteracy found in many underdeveloped nations is not conducive to extensive horizons. Secondly, he asserts, inter-nation intercourse demands certain organizational skills and capabilities which may be lacking in less-developed countries; and finally, the functional interests of developed and underdeveloped nations may be quite different. Etzioni notes in particular the preoccupation of underdeveloped countries with domestic problems.

Proposition 11b—The greater their homogeneity in terms of internal development, the more two nations will tend to interact.

Issue may be taken with the notion that average level of development is the most salient. The common problems shared by developing nations and the common desire to break old dependency relations would tend to serve as a basis for mutual identifications among underdeveloped nations. This, coupled with the urgency of their needs, may lead them to seek cooperative solutions among themselves (Nye, Povolny). The East African and Central American common markets are cases in point. This notion of shared functional interests leads to the hypothesis that homogeneity in internal development might influence with whom a state would interact.

Proposition 11c—Internal development will have no net effect on the patterns of interaction between states.

Both of the above propositions are confounded by the fact that historically, colonial ties, to say nothing of strategic Cold War considerations, have left close relational ties between many developed and underdeveloped nations (Deutsch, 1960b). The net impact may be that in the aggregate, the degree of internal development within a nation-pair will bear no relation to the scope and intensity of interaction.

(6) INTERNAL POLITICAL STABILITY

Proposition 12a—The greater the average level of regime stability, the more those two nations will tend to interact.

The most obvious hypothesis links stability with inter-nation intercourse. This follows quite naturally from a consideration of the sort of mutual predictability and responsive capabilities arising from the continuity of political regimes and the demands for intensive and extensive contacts with other nations. Many theorists seem to subscribe to this hypothesis (Ake, Liska), and ample evidence may be garnered in their behalf. For example, Etzioni (1965) notes that both the Republic of the Congo and Brazil were so overwhelmed with internal political problems in the early 1960's that neither could afford to devote much in the way of attention and resources to external affairs.

Proposition 12b—The more heterogeneous two nations in terms of regime stability, the more those two nations will tend to interact.

In contrast, Burton, in an opinion shared by Liska, argues that political instability may itself be a possible reason for seeking external relations. Faultering national leaders may be able to prop up their regimes by establishing intense relations with more stable nations. Burton contends that many domestically unstable governments have been able to sustain themselves in this way owing in no small part to the receptiveness for this kind of arrangement on the part of status-quo nations such as the United States.

Proposition 12c—The more homogeneous two nations in terms of regime stability, the more those two nations will tend to interact.

From the standpoint of functional interests, we may offer yet another seemingly viable hypothesis. To reverse a notion posited by Deutsch (1959) and Guetzkow (1957), internal political instability may reflect an instability of a state to go it alone, and such instability will lead to efforts to find solutions to mutual problems through cooperation with similarly unstable nations.

(7) MILITARY POWER

Students of the so-called realist school of international relations universally find military power to be a crucial determinant of international behavior (Morgenthau, 1967; Organski).

Proposition 13a—The greater and more similar the military capabilities of two nations, the more those two nations will tend to interact.

Organski conceptualizes interstate intercourse in terms of a pyramid in which states of similar capabilities tend to interact. J. Galtung (1966) contends that the greater the similarity and the higher the average level of two nations in terms of military strength, the greater the ensuing collaboration.

Proposition 13b—The more heterogeneous two nations with respect to military power, the more those two nations will tend to interact.

However, many students of alliance behavior tend to dispute the above contentions. Liska, Morgenthau (1959), and Wolfers argue that militarily weaker states will seek to augment their security by establishing ties with a stronger power and that dominant powers will tend to be responsive to these efforts mainly to prevent the resources of the small nations from falling into the realm of a potential adversary. Insofar, then, as the vulnerability of a state is greater, the weaker it is militarily; and its vulnerability can be overcome through ties with a stronger nation.

The small-groups literature suggests that the tendency will give rise to a communications pattern which Guetzkow and Simon characterize as a "wheel." This is to say, there will be greater interaction between militarily stronger and weaker nations than among weaker nations themselves. Wolfers contends that such a "wheel-like" structure can, in fact, be found in the Soviet and American alliances. Brody in a simulation study finds such a manifest pattern between nuclear and nonnuclear nations.

(8) ECONOMIC POWER

Many theorists suggest an implicit link between economic capability and propensity to interact.

> Proposition 14a—The greater the average economic capability of two nations, the more those two nations will tend to interact.

> Proposition 14b—The more homogeneous two nations with regard to economic capabilities, the more those two nations will tend to interact.

The link between average economic capability and interaction is suggested by several empirical studies (J. Galtung, 1966; E. Haas, 1958; Organski; Rummel, 1968; E. Haas and Schmitter). However, others stress the homogeneity of the economic capability of the nation-pair. Etzioni (1965) suggests the European Economic Community, the Latin American Free Trade Area, and the various African customs unions "are composed of countries fairly similar in their economies to one another" (20). To reinforce his argument, he alludes to the fact that economic heterogeneity contributed to Katanga's secessionist drive from the Republic of the Congo, to Senegal's break from the Federation of Mali, and to Gabon's initial reluctance to join a Central African customs union (22).

> Proposition 14c—The more heterogeneous two nations with respect to economic capabilities, the more those two nations will tend to interact.

Schmitter warns, however, that the key is not the absolute level of economic power, but the relative level of one nation compared to another. In this instance, an argument in favor of heterogeneity as a predictor of nation-pair interaction could be advanced. The basis for the contention is simply that nations with high economic capacities seek markets and raw resources in countries with less economic productivity and fewer processing capabilities. Industrialized economies tend to complement agrarian and single-product economies. However, cursory empirical evidence tends to support the reverse of this notion (i.e., Proposition 14b).

(9) BUREAUCRATIC, OR ADMINISTRATIVE, CAPABILITIES

The final unit property to be considered relates to the bureaucratic capacities of nation-states.

> **Proposition 15a—The greater and more homogeneous the bureaucratic capabilities of two nations, the more those two nations will tend to interact.**

As was discussed earlier, international intercourse does not occur without a price. Certain burdens, or loads, are placed on the participating nations. The pattern of interaction between two nations is therefore dependent upon and limited by their respective political and administrative capabilities (Deutsch, 1954). One is not surprised, then, that Deutsch and his colleagues (1957) find well-developed institutional capabilities among those conditions they deem essential for a security community, amalgamated or pluralistic. Russett (1963, 1965) also emphasizes the importance of organization, or bureaucratic capabilities, in establishing and maintaining mutually responsive and enduring ties between nations. Although less explicit in assessing its impact, Organski, likewise, finds the bureaucratic capability of a nation to be an important determinant of its external relations.

The concept of mutual responsiveness as it relates to bureaucratic capabilities seems to imply two things: 1) a high average level of bureaucratic development and 2) homogeneity of bureaucratic capacity. The former suggests that burdens of inter-nation communication or interaction need not necessarily be distributed evenly, while the latter argues that such intercourse is facilitated by comparable capabilities. We are inclined to view the two aspects as complementary and, therefore, the two-part hypothesis stated above.

Although we know of no literature which explicitly supports the proposition, for the sake of theoretical completeness we offer the following null counterpart:

> **Proposition 15b—Level and homogeneity of administrative capability has no relationship to relative interaction between states.**

Systemic Properties   The third and final set of background factors to be considered are systemic properties, those arising from past patterns of interaction and collaboration. These properties, we have argued, are indicative of past habits and memories of attention as well as current capabilities stemming from previous institutional arrangements designed to facilitate interaction. Our general hypothesis is that previous collaboration has relevance to ensuing patterns of mutual interaction.

PREVIOUS COLLABORATIVE EXPERIENCE

Etzioni (1967) argues that community is not a static phenomenon which characterizes relations among nations, but is a reflection of a continual process developing over time and ultimately passing a threshold which he characterizes as "integration." As a result, in looking at what elements will contribute to present indicators of cohesion, the investigator must examine prior patterns of collaboration.

Proposition 16a—Nations will be more likely to develop attitudinal and transactional ties if they have collaborated previously.

If mutual relevance can be viewed as including favorable mass perceptions as well as an exchange of goods, people, etc., then prior interaction such as tourism and exchange of students creates a greater degree of understanding and friendliness among masses of various countries and a greater tolerance for foreign customs (I. Galtung, 265–275; Pool, 1965). Collaboration over a number of decades between Norway and Sweden eventually has led to more reciprocal positive affect between the national masses (Lindgren).

On the relationship between prior collaboration and ensuing interaction, relationships between nations over time may become regularized and even formalized. This phenomenon is often explained in terms of sociopsychological learning mechanisms (Teune). In Guetzkow's words (1957), "The more satisfactorily group members have been able to solve their past problems through intergroup relations, the more likely they are to collaborate with other groups when new needs arise" (51).

In the context of empirical studies, Lipjhart (257) analyzes transaction flows in Western Europe and finds that those countries which had the highest rates of exchanges were those with a history characterized by recurrent collaboration; this is particularly noteworthy among the Scandinavian and Common Market countries. In another study with a global emphasis, Brams (1967, 1–18) finds that Commonwealth ties mean that former British colonies in Africa are just as likely to trade with members of the Commonwealth now as with other countries in Africa; prior trading with Britain and other former colonies is more important than responding to pleas for more intraregional trading in Africa.

This proposition seems to provide the central premise underlying the functional theory of international organization (E. Haas, 1964; Mitrany). The argument runs briefly as follows: mutually rewarding collaboration will tend to "spill-over" into other areas and foster greater interaction and collaboration in the future (E. Haas, 1964). In a sense, interaction may be seen as self-generative. Following from the above, a reasonable assertion would appear to be that the extent of past collaboration is a measure of the satisfaction accruing from that collaboration.

Proposition 16b—Nations are not more likely to develop close attitudinal and transactional ties if they have cooperated in the past.

Plausible as the first proposition seems, it is confounded by the fact that intercourse can lead to disillusionment as well as satisfaction (Deutsch, 1964b). As Teune has observed, "The plausible explanation that interaction leads to favorable attitudes is contradicted by the explanatory observation that familiarity breeds contempt" (261). Moreover, even if interaction should prove satisfactory, inasmuch as it is purposive behavior, predication is not only based on the economic satisfaction of its purpose but also on the continued existence of these purposes. Collaboration between governments may take the form of little more than paper agreements, having little or no effect on the actual behavior of the parties involved.

Empirical assessments of the propositions are limited in number and in scope. Russett (1963) asserts that after more than a century of close cooperation, there is little evidence of attitudinal ties or transactional growth between the United States and Great Britain, as this dyad has been stultified for some time. Similarly, but in a much more impressionistic manner, Hoffman asserts that the United States and France have had a history of collaboration in forms of military and economic alignments, yet mutual relevance in terms of attitudes or transactions has reached the point of decay. How these conflicting hypotheses would fare in a more systematic examination at either the regional or global level remains to be seen. For the present, both the postulated link between previous collaboration and subsequent intercourse and its null counterpart will be entertained.

From Mutual Relevance to Formal Intergovernmental Collaboration   Having discussed the relationships between background factors and the patterns of relative interaction between nations which we take to indicate their mutual relevance, we may now turn to the second major linkage prescribed by our model, the linkage between mutual relevance and formal intergovernmental collaboration.

One of the consequences of a high level of transactional exchange[25] between publics such as tourism and trade is an increase in intergovernmental collaboration.

Proposition 17—The level of transactional exchange among states is highly correlated with intergovernmental collaboration.

As we have previously noted, the fact that patterns of interaction establish the mutual relevance of two nations does not necessarily mean that they will be productive of positive sentiment. Most scholars, however, tend to be optimistic in their assessments of the effects of personal contact; Russett's reasoning (1965) is perhaps typical:

> On the whole, contact results in a degree of sympathy or affection for the other culture or nation, or if not affection, at least understanding for some of the basic concerns and needs of its people. Or if we cannot say even that much, we can conclude that *without* substantial personal contact two nations whose fates are closely intertwined, and who must frequently act upon each other at the governmental level, are very unlikely to be very responsive to each other's needs. That is, contact alone may not produce responsiveness, but it is difficult to have sustained responsiveness without it [39].

Etzioni (1965, 229–284) asserts that governments react to personal and commodity exchange by becoming cooperative with those governments with whom interaction is high. The principal form of the governmental response is in the signing of agreements, either conventions, treaties or exchange of diplomatic notes.[26] Etzioni has no empirical data, but asserts that the supranational flurry of activity in Western Europe during the late 1950's, with accompanying treaty signatures, is a consequence of high transaction rates among the participating countries.

In a subsequent volume, Etzioni (1966) lends further support to this position. He points out that the transition from formal intergovernmental arrangements to self-sustaining patterns of inter-nation intercourse

25. A distinction is made between transactions which take a nongovernmental form of cooperation such as mail, tourism, and student exchange; and governmental collaboration which takes the form of some formalized type of agreement such as a treaty or a convention.
26. For a discussion of the various characteristics of these different forms of agreement, see Starke (1950).

is infrequent and unlikely. The process tends to operate in the opposite direction. The central factor promoting formal collaboration and the institutionalization of relations, he writes, is

> the amount of decision-making called for by inter-country flows and by shared performance that, in turn, is determined by the scope of tasks carried out internationally. . . . The central variables . . . is the amount of international decision-making required. This, in turn, is determined by the amounts and kinds of flows that cross the international borders and the amounts and kinds of shared international activities [40].

Another empirical study of Western Europe documents the same trend. Russett (1963) examines Anglo-American relations over the past four decades on a variety of indicators from transactions to intergovernmental pacts. All of the transaction variables on the nongovernmental level such as mail, migration, trade, and tourism reached a peak in magnitude in the late 1930's or early 1940's and steadily declined until 1958. Russett asserts that capabilities in terms of transaction levels were lower in the 1950's than any other time in the preceding seventy years.

In the level of governmental cooperation between the United States and Britain, the last seventy years were examined to determine if there was congruence with transactional indicators. Collaboration in terms of signing pacts peaked immediately preceding and following the the the outbreak of World War II. In the ensuing decades, the number of agreements signed by both declined. The convergence of transactions and pacts leads Russett (1963, 81–127, 162–195) to conclude that responsiveness between these countries has been reduced sharply over the last two decades.

Another study stressing the congruence between transactions and formalized agreements is an investigation by Simon (32–36) of Communist bloc members of Eastern Europe and newly developing nations.[27] Using trade as a transactional measure, Simon finds a correlation of .63 with the number of treaties signed per dyad; other transactions such as student exchange (.47) are not as highly interrelated with treaty signings, but the only types of agreements considered were those concerning military commitments. This is a narrow treatment, ignoring other spheres of governmental collaboration.

In describing the time lag between expansion of transactional exchange and its ultimate impact on governmental collaboration, Etzioni argues that the influence is reciprocal. However, the exchanges on the nongovernmental level will be more likely to have their impact shown in a shorter period of time as governmental decision-makers act to formalize nongovernmental interactions quickly by signing agreements. For ex-

---

27. The Communist bloc states in Simon's study included the Soviet Union, Bulgaria, Czechoslovakia, Hungary, Poland, Rumania, and Yugoslavia. The newly developing states included such countries as India and Egypt.

ample, a treaty to ease obstacles to tourism between two countries could be the result of exchanges of large numbers of tourists. The speed of a governmental response will be more rapid if exchange is high on more than one indicator. An example would be the Benelux area, where numerous agreements signed reflects nongovernmental cooperation of many forms.

However, in examining the impact of governmental agreements on transactions, the time lag will be longer since treaties must be enacted and a given time must elapse before the components of the agreement are enforced (Etzioni, 1967, 38–51). Several years passed between the initial signing of pacts leading to the creation of Treaty of Rome and the eventual impetus given to transactional exchange (Lindberg).

Commenting on the relationship between transactions and inter-governmental collaboration, Deutsch (1954) proposes an analogy between inter-nation transaction flows and the traffic load at an intersection of roads. Just as formal facilities—policemen, traffic lights, etc.—are required for the movement and control of traffic, formal or institutional mechanisms are required in international intercourse. These must keep pace with the volume of transaction and adjustment problems thrown upon them as mutual relevance increases. Thus, formal collaboration may be viewed as a vehicle for mutual problem-solving and as such, a function of the need and desire to sustain and/or expand responsive sentiments.

These arguments are further underlined and complemented by Guetzkow's contention (1957) that collaboration stems, in part, from past successes and satisfactions in relational endeavors. While Guetzkow rejects the "notion that sheer contact between nations necessarily produces collaboration" (50), the basic hypothesis seems to suggest that a nation's past relational experience will be reflected in the scope and intensity of its current patterns of interaction. This, in turn, suggests that the more mutually relevant two nations, the more likely they are to collaborate.

Morgenthau (1959) also seems to concur with the conclusion that mutual relevance tends to lead to formal collaboration. Speaking of military collaboration in particular, he contends that formal agreements are much more likely where a "community of interest" is involved. Insofar as we may take mutual relevance as indicative of a community of interest, this is but a specific case of our general argument.

Mirroring many of the views of Deutsch, Jacob provides the basis of yet another argument which tends to reinforce the conclusion that mutual relevance tends to precede formal collaboration. He notes that political decision-makers tend to act within the constraints of prevailing patterns of accepted behavior. They rarely buck informally established norms and often seek policy rationalization in these norms. With slight extension, this suggests that formal intergovernmental collaboration may, at times, serve simply to symbolically legitimize extant patterns of intercourse.

Formal collaboration, then, may be seen both as a response to challenges, past and present, and as evidence of past relational successes. Increasing mutual relevance between nations tends to result in such a formal arrangement to more effectively cope with the interaction in order to insure its continuance and promote its expansion, to assure its legitimacy, and to provide security for the common interests involved.

Finally, the functional arguments to include the spill-over notions of E. Haas are also relevant. An optimistic conclusion stresses that interaction breeds collaboration. However, the relationship between nongovernmental and governmental forms of cooperation has yet to be investigated rigorously for a number of countries in either a regional or a global setting.

In presenting the model which serves as the framework for this study, we suggested that the relationship between formal collaboration and informal interaction was probably reciprocal to some extent. But we are inclined to see the primary flow of influence from mutual relevance, defined by relative patterns of informal interaction, to patterns of intergovernmental collaboration.

The Relationship Between a Supranational Institutional Structure and Ensuing Attitudinal Integration

Another aspect of the reciprocal relationship between indicators of mutual salience and governmental collaboration reflecting the nature of the feedback concerns the extent to which institutional impact changes mass attitudes. Deutsch and his associates (1957, 3–9) argue that one of the steps leading to the development of an integrated community is the creation of supranational institutions. In the North Atlantic community, a key occurrence was the creation of the Common Market in 1958 and the Free Trade area. Such organizational developments provide an impetus to greater popular support for more efforts at unification as well as lead to a more favorable perception of other nations in the area (Etzioni, 1965).

Proposition 18a—In any region following the creation of supranational institutions, there must be a stronger commitment to the affective and action components of attitudinal integration.

In viewing public opinion polls over a decade in France, Great Britain, West Germany, and Italy, Puchala concludes that after the creation of the supranational structure in Western Europe, there has been a marked increase in support of a united Europe. While there is as yet no desire to lose national sovereignty in exchange for a regional union, there is general acceptance of the notion of European collaboration (Puchala, 1966, 1–10; Gallup International, 101–126).

This position is supported by a recent study of the attitudes of young people in the age bracket from sixteen to nineteen in France, West Germany, the Netherlands, and Britain. In comparing the results of the youth sample with a general sample of all age groups,[28] there is greater support for European unification among those under twenty-one than in any other age group. The attitudes of the youth do not appear to be superficial, but knowledgeable and resistant to change. Not only have efforts to achieve unity made great strides, but the pace will be accelerated once these youths attain political maturity and begin participating in their nations' political affairs.

One key variable differentiating youth and older age groups is knowledge of the activities of European supranational institutions. Older people have not aged in a time when supranational activities played a preeminent role in national politics. Consequently, when people cognizant of organizational activities mature, there will be an even greater impetus toward European unification (Inglehart, 91–105).

> **Proposition 18b—In any region following the creation of supranational institutions, there will not be a stronger commitment to the affective and action components of attitudinal integration.**

However, there is opposition to the linkage between supranational activities and ensuing changes in attitudes. Russett (1965, 46–54) finds that the British public has not become more receptive to the French and West Germans since 1958, as less positive affect has been generated in the late 1960's than in the late 1950's. Klineberg (108–109) asserts that all national masses support the status quo; his prime evidence comes from opinion polls regarding domestic issues.[29] The impact on mass attitudes of supranational activity as it occurred in Western Europe in the late 1950's can be subjected to further examination.

Conclusion   In this chapter, we have considered a number of propositions relating to the general relationships posited in our model in the study of inter-nation collaboration. The arguments we have presented are drawn largely from the contemporary

28. The age groups were 16–19, 21–29, 30–39, 40–50, and over 50.
29. Examples of issues are attitudes toward capital punishment in West Germany and opinions regarding desegregation in the United States.

literature on international relations. We make no claim, however, of doing justice to the profundity of thought and insight contained within the work upon which we have drawn. For purposes of our analysis we have found it necessary to reduce complex and often elaborate arguments to a relatively simple set of behavioral hypotheses. The analytic advantages gained from such simplification and abstraction will hopefully pave the way for more sophisticated analyses.

The specific hypotheses that have been outlined here seek to explain international patterns of mutual relevance at three distinct levels of explanation: geophysical, systemic, and subsystemic. Behaviorally defined patterns of mutual relevance are, in turn, linked to patterns of inter-governmental collaborative behavior. In addition, the feedback of col-laborative indicators on elements of mutual relevance such as transactions and attitudes is also discussed. In reviewing the arguments regarding these relationships, we have found the literature rife with apparently contradictory contentions. As in the proverbs of folklore, we suspect that there is a glimmer of insight in all of these contentions. What we seek to establish is not the truth in any absolute sense, but general behavioral tendencies. This we think can serve as a precursor to a better empirical understanding of a phenomenal world that seems to tolerate substantial contradiction. Once general tendencies have been identified, we should be better prepared to isolate and explore deviant patterns of behavior.

PART II

THE NATURE OF
THE EMPIRICAL
STUDIES

chapter 4

Research Design
and Data Acquisition

Introduction   Before the hypotheses detailed in the last
chapter can be subjected to rigorous empirical
scrutiny, a number of methodological and technical problems must be
discussed. The basic unit of analysis must be identified, observations
selected, and abstract concepts concretized. Attention must also be given
to procedures of data collection and analysis. These considerations mark
the concerns of this chapter.

Selection of   A decision was made to examine two levels
the Sample   of community formation in terms of the
model postulated in Chapter 2. Since the lit-
erature on integration has been focused on either a regional or a global
basis, we might attempt to systematically investigate community formation in both contexts. We examined the relationships posited in the
previous chapter to determine if there was any congruence in propositions
concerning collaboration at a subsystemic and systemic level.
The usage of studies with different foci has various advantages.
There are different theoretical gains in each strategy, and insights can
be gained by employing both forms of analysis instead of relying on just
one mode of analysis. Relations which might be obscured in one context

may be more clearly delineated in another mode. For example, if geographic proximity has no predictive power in the North Atlantic area, but appears salient in the global study, one could argue that the American separation from other proximate North Atlantic nations in a small study was responsible for the low set of correlations. However, in a larger study, where most of the nations are not proximate (i.e., not the case in the North Atlantic region) and not removed from a single dominant nation, then propinquity will emerge as a salient predictor.

In choosing a regional sample, the North Atlantic area was selected for a variety of reasons. First, the phenomenon of building a supranational community has reached a level in the Atlantic region which has not been attained elsewhere. The rise of communities such as the Common Market has been a major development of the post–World War II world and an understanding of the dynamics of this process will provide valuable insights into similar occurrences in other areas. Secondly, many of the notions underlying integration theory have been developed in this area. However, most of the research has been speculative without using rigorous research procedures, and an empirical study dealing with a number of countries in a systematic fashion appears possible and useful. Thirdly, the North Atlantic area is the only region where data is available on mass perceptions of other nations over the last fifteen years for a variety of countries. Complete information does not even exist for most other countries in the attitudinal realm as far back as 1950. Thus, a study outside Europe would be fraught with unreliable estimates (Simon).

In selecting a sample, an effort was made to approximate Deutsch and his associates' list of nineteen countries in the seminal study of the area.[1] After a preliminary search for relevant information, fifteen countries were selected as likely sources for opinion and transaction data: Austria, Belgium, Canada, Denmark, Finland, France, German Federal Republic, Great Britain, Italy, The Netherlands, Norway, Spain, Sweden, Switzerland, and the United States.[2]

In selecting a sample for the global system, the criterion employed was data availability on as wide a variety of transaction measures as possible. No attempt was made to gather attitudinal data, since efforts to garner relevant perceptual data would be frustrated if the search was expanded beyond Western Europe. A sample of forty-nine nations was selected with nations from all regions of the world. The list, organized by region, is found in Table 4.1.

---

1. For the countries in this study, see Deutsch, et al., 1957, 10.
2. Henceforth "North Atlantic" will refer to the above fifteen nations.

Selection of the   In the past, most research in the purview of
Unit of Analysis   international relations has focused on the
                    nation-state as the unit of analysis. This has
meant that studies stress the characteristics of individual nations to determine their capacity in wielding power (Snyder). However, in recent
years, attention has been shifted to supranational units in an attempt to
cope with the dynamics of interaction between national entities. One of
the more frequently used units of analysis is the dyad, or nation-pair,
particularly in the area of integration research where relations among
states have been the pivot for inquiry (Brody; Rummel; Russett, 1963;
1965). The dyad was selected as the best approach for the study owing
to the focus on cooperative behavior and perceptions of national masses.

However, two different approaches to dyadic analysis were undertaken in this study. In the North Atlantic area, a "directional dyad" was
utilized in that any given nation-pair accounts for two separate observations. This was employed to take account of discrepancies between dyad
partners. Attitudinal data can be most usefully employed in this framework. Perceptions of others are not necessarily reciprocal, as Americans
may perceive Germans with considerable negative effect, while Germans
believe that Americans are friendly (Deutsch and Edinger).

In the instance of the North Atlantic area, 210 directional dyads
were involved, with all the countries mentioned in the earlier North

TABLE 4.1

The Forty-Nine Nations Comprising the Global Sample

Canada	France	Soviet Union
United States	German Federal Republic	Yugoslavia
Mexico	Greece	Israel
Panama	Ireland	Iran
Argentina	Italy	Iraq
Bolivia	Netherlands	Lebanon
Brazil	Norway	Syria
Chile	Portugal	United Arab Republic
Colombia	Spain	South Africa
Peru	Sweden	India
Uruguay	Switzerland	Indonesia
Venezuela	Turkey	Japan
Austria	United Kingdom	Pakistan
Belgium–Luxembourg	Czechoslovakia	Philippines
Denmark	Hungary	Thailand
Finland	Poland	Australia
		New Zealand

Atlantic study (Deutsch et al., 1957) included. A directional dyad would be France–Italy or vice versa. Each nation-pair would constitute two directional dyads, or two separate entries per nation-pair. An example is as follows: the number of letters sent from France to Italy would not necessarily be the same as the number sent from Italy to France.[3] In this study, both would be recorded as separate observations. However, with respect to the attitudinal data, lack of information limited consideration of propositions concerning attitudinal variables to fifty-two dyads. These fifty-two attitudinal directional dyads are listed in Table 4.2.

TABLE 4.2

*The Fifty-Two Directional Dyads With Relevant Opinion Data
In The North Atlantic Sample*

Austria–France	G.F.R.–Italy
Austria–G.F.R. (German Federal Republic)	G.F.R.–United States
Austria–Great Britain	Great Britain–France
Austria–Italy	Great Britain–G.F.R.
Austria–United States	Great Britain–Italy
Belgium–France	Great Britain–United States
Belgium–G.F.R.	Italy–France
Belgium–Great Britain	Italy–G.F.R.
Belgium–Italy	Italy–Great Britain
Belgium–Spain	Italy–United States
Belgium–United States	Netherlands–France
Canada–France	Netherlands–G.F.R.
Canada–G.F.R.	Netherlands–Great Britain
Canada–United States	Netherlands–Sweden
Denmark–France	Netherlands–United States
Denmark–G.F.R.	Norway–Denmark
Denmark–Great Britain	Norway–France
Denmark–Italy	Norway–G.F.R.
Denmark–Norway	Norway–Great Britain
Denmark–United States	Norway–Italy
France–G.F.R.	Norway–United States
France–Great Britain	Spain–United States
France–Italy	United States–France
France–United States	United States–G.F.R.
G.F.R.–France	United States–Great Britain
G.F.R.–Great Britain	United States–Italy

The first nation listed is the national mass which perceives another nation and the second is the object of the perception.

3. The formula for the number of directional dyads is $N(N-1)$ or in this instance $15(14) = 210$.

In the global study, a different approach was utilized. A "summed dyad" was chosen as the unit of analysis with one entry per nation-pair. This choice arose from a concern for measuring the "responsiveness" of two nations in terms of their total interaction on a variety of measures regardless of initiator. With a total of forty-nine nations, there were 1176 observations per variable.[4]

In neither study was the group selected to constitute a random sampling of the North Atlantic region or the world. Although an effort was made to obtain as wide a geographical distribution in the global system and as complete a sample in the regional study as possible, a key in the basis of selection was data availability.

As these criteria are not conducive to the assumption of broader representativeness, the results of our analysis are assumed to describe only the dyads considered. This means that statistical measures are to be interpreted as descriptive rather than inferential statistics. In other words, our statistics cannot be considered unbiased estimates of parameters for a larger population, but serve only as summary descriptive measures of variables and variable relationships across the dyads under study.

Formal tests of statistical significance are, therefore, inappropriate. Nevertheless, we report values of the relevant measures of association at the .05 two-tailed probability levels under the assumptions of the inferential statistic. This is done simply for the convenience of the reader who may want to entertain the possibility that these variable relationships are more broadly representative.

Operational The hypotheses developed in Chapter 3 con-
Definitions and tain concepts that might be called quasi-
Major Data Sources operational. The phenomenal referents of the
hypotheses are fairly clear. Still, the concepts involved do little more than point to a range of concrete phenomena. Systematic empirical investigation demands more. Specific variables must be identified and measurement procedures prescribed. In other words, the concepts must be defined operationally.

Once this is done, a researcher is prepared to face the hard task of data acquisition. This tends to pose a major problem in the study of international relations. In comparison to other areas of political science, work in international relations has suffered from a dearth of empirical inquiry. This paucity of empirical study stems from many sources, not the least of which is the scarcity of readily available data. Recent efforts designed to

---

4. The formula for the number of summed dyads is $N(N-1)/2$. Thus, India and Australia would have a summed total per variable such as mail exchange.

help remedy this situation (Banks and Textor; Rummel et al.; Russett et al.) have provided succor for empirically oriented students of international relations. Nonetheless, the store of quantitative data remains meager in comparison to the needs of the field. This is particularly true as one moves from cross-national to international research.

The data demands of the present study thus led us into rather virgin territory and necessitated considerable improvisation. Given the quantity of data required, it is probably not surprising that data collection and its reduction to the desired form proved the most troublesome and time-consuming aspect of the study.

The data required by the operational definitions outlined below were obtained from numerous sources. Whenever possible, an effort was made to use existing data banks. In the following discussion, we note the major sources of data for each of the variables. A detailed listing of all sources is provided in the Bibliography under "Data Sources."

Following the general model outlined in Chapter 2, we will first consider operational definitions and measures of the three types of background factors and then move to consider the empirical meanings to be attached to the concepts of mutual relevance and intergovernmental collaboration.

(1) Background Factors: Geophysical Properties   Three distinct types of background factors have been identified as potential wellsprings of international behavior. The first of these are geophysical properties. The concept of interest is geographical proximity.

To tap this concept, two measures are used. The first is the great circle distance between the capital or major city in one nation and that of the other. The primary source for these data was the International Air Transport Association's *Tabulation of Great Circle Distances*, obtained through the good offices of the *Encyclopaedia Britannica*.

In and of itself, great circle distance is probably not sufficient to capture the meaning of geographical proximity. As was previously observed, a number of scholars have attached particular importance to the role of territorial contiguity. Accordingly, this aspect of geographical proximity is measured through a pseudovariable marking the presence or absence of a shared boundary. These observations were obtained from inspection of standards maps from the United States Coast and Geodetic Survey.

These two variables (viz., capital-to-capital distance and common boundaries) are then taken collectively to indicate geographical proximity. The relative weightings of the two variables are determined inductively through procedures to be discussed presently.

(2) *Background* The background predictors for both studies
Factors: Unit, or are discussed in this segment. All of the ele-
Societal, Properties ments discussed below are included in some
form in the global study. However, most are
excluded from the regional study because there would be little variation
between countries, as the area is highly homogeneous on most of the
background indicators, especially when compared with other areas of
the world. As a result, the focus in the North Atlantic area is on attitudes
or values and prior expectations in terms of wartime experience.

We are interested in two types of analytic properties arising from
the internal characteristics of the nations in each dyad. The first relates
to the extent to which the two nations share, or are homogeneous with
respect to, a given background attribute; the second, to the average level,
or magnitude, of the attribute present in and characterizing the dyad. To
clarify this distinction, consider some internal variable, for instance,
bureaucratic development. Take two dyads, say the United States–United
Kingdom and Thailand–Indonesia. Both of these dyads are relatively
homogeneous with respect to the level of internal bureaucratic development. But in terms of the average, or mean, level of bureaucratic development, the two dyads are markedly different, the United States–United
Kingdom possessing much more highly developed bureaucracies. The
hypotheses we have proposed suggest that either or both of these types
of dyadic characteristics may be important.

In general, attribute homogeneity is measured by 100 times the
ratio of the attribute in one nation to that in another, the smaller value
always being in the numerator. Expressed formally, Homo $A_i = 100
\times (A_{ij}/A_{ik})$, where $A_{ij} \leqq A_{ik}$. To avoid the problems stemming from
the peculiar characteristics of zero dividends (i.e., $0 \div n = 0$, for all
$n \neq 0$), a constant (1) was added to all items of scales that varied from
zero. Individual measures of attribute homogeneity thus will have maximum values of 100 and *approach* 0 as heterogeneity increases. Attribute
density (i.e., the level or magnitude of an attribute within a dyad), is
measured simply by the mean value of the attribute present in the two
nations forming the dyad.

In most cases, a multiple measure is ultimately used to index a
concept. This overall measure is arrived at through an optimally weighted
linear additive function of the relevant measures of either attribute
homogeneity or attribute density. The weightings assigned to the vari-

ables in such composite measures are arrived at inductively using a "best predictor" criterion discussed later in this chapter. Exceptions to the above procedures will be noted in the context of the specific operationalizations that follow.

HOMOGENEITY OF POLITICAL VALUES: THE GLOBAL STUDY

The operative political values of a nation are tapped through three variables. The first is a three-point "freedom of opposition" scale. The scale is taken from the Dimensionality of Nations (DON) project and ranges from "no political opposition allowed" to "mostly unrealistic political opposition" (see Rummel, 1964). The second, also from DON, is a three-point "press censorship" scale, running from "complete or fairly complete censorship" to "no censorship." The third variable is total Communist party membership. As for the previous two measures, data on this variable was obtained from the DON project. Individual homogeneity measures based on these three variables are used collectively to index dyadic homogeneity of values.

HOMOGENEITY OF POLITICAL VALUES: THE REGIONAL STUDY

Another aspect of the value cluster, other than societal practices, which is scrutinized in the North Atlantic study is the salience of certain key attitudinal dimensions which characterize mass perceptions of other nations and efforts toward achieving greater integration. Deutsch (1957) asserted that there were two key aspects of attitudinal integration: friendliness and good feeling toward others, and support of policies designed to achieve greater regional unification. In terms of the former aspect, or the affective component, an appropriate measure would be the extent to which people of one country had good or bad feelings toward other specific countries. The question which was asked was, "Please tell me your feelings about various countries. How about _____?" Responses were coded as *good feelings, bad feelings, indifferent,* or *don't know.* Only those recorded as ascribing "good feelings" toward others were considered to meet the affective component.[5]

This question was asked repetitively over time in polls sponsored

5. An aid in finding the same questions asked in different countries was that most countries in the area have an affiliate of the Gallup Poll which standardizes many of its questions in different countries. For a list of the polling agencies used in Europe, see Bibliography under "Data Sources."

by the United States Information Agency and undertaken by reputable polling agencies over the last decade and a half in four nations, France, the German Federal Republic, Great Britain, and Italy. In addition, the same question was asked at different times in several other countries and there were only three countries, Finland, Sweden, and Switzerland, on which no data was gathered on the affective component. No other question was asked repetitively over time in more than one country.

The second aspect of attitudinal integration was the support of policies aiding regional integration. This "policy component"[6] of mass attitudes could be found in the following query, "Are you in general for or against making efforts toward uniting Western Europe?" This question or a facsimile[7] was asked over the past fifteen years in most countries of the North Atlantic area except the United States, Canada, Finland, and Spain.[8] There were other questions in opinion polls involving policy ramifications of Western unity efforts such as the expansion of the Common Market, but data was found for only a few countries with limited time-spans.[9] As a result, attitudinal integration will be viewed as having two components, the affective component, in terms of perceptions of other countries, and the policy component, or support for efforts toward expanding Western European unification.[10]

The opinion data was gathered from two sources: polls under the auspices of the United States Information Agency (USIA) and surveys from polling agencies within the respective countries. The former has conducted periodic polls in France, Great Britain, Italy, and West Germany. Every several months, the surveys were administered by polls located in the various countries and have been used as indicators of attitudinal integration (Deutsch, 1960a; Merritt and Puchala; Russett, 1965).

In addition, questions concerning the affective and policy components of mass opinion have been asked in various North Atlantic countries by indigenous polling agencies as part of their own polling duties. These polls have been collected by the Roper Public Opinion

6. This was earlier named the "action component," but the new term was selected to avoid any confusion with actual action, since only advocacy of a policy was evinced.

7. In some instances, the question said "political unification" of Western Europe, but distributions on such queries were not drastically altered.

8. There had to be at least two separate opinion samplings in two different years to be included.

9. In most instances, information was limited to Common Market countries since 1958. Distributions were similar (i.e., within ten percentage points) on such questions as on unity queries.

10. Only those advocating further unification were considered to be integrative on the policy component.

Center (Bisco; Hastings). In most instances, relevant questions were asked only once every three or four years in contrast to the more periodic polling in the surveys administered by the Information Agency. The year 1952 was selected as the beginning point for the study because opinion data was unavailable prior to that time for all countries other than the United States and Canada. Opinion data was obtained for all countries in the sample except Finland, Sweden, and Switzerland.[11]

One problem which has developed in attitude studies over time is the wording of questions. The problem is not of paramount importance in this study with questions only on feelings toward other countries and attitudes toward European unity. Both questions were worded in a similar fashion, but were there others which might reflect relevant attitudes? In most cases similar questions were not asked.[12] The one exception was in the polls of the United States Information Agency, as a query dealt with the trustworthiness of other nations. The responses to this question were highly correlated with the answers to the friendliness question as indicated by a Pearson product-moment correlation of .75.

CULTURAL HOMOGENEITY

Three composite submeasures are used to index cultural homogeneity. The first of these is language homogeneity. As defined in this study, it is derived from the summed percentage differences between two nations in terms of persons speaking each of seven different languages, English, French, German, Spanish–Portuguese, Russian, Chinese–Japanese, and Arabic. The specific formula is

$$LH = 100 - (\sum_{i=1}^{7} /L_{ij} - L_{ik}/)/2,$$

where LH represents language homogeneity; L_{ij}, the percentage of the population of nation j speaking language i; and L_{ik}, the percentage of nation k speaking language i.

The second variable used in indexing cultural homogeneity is a composite measure of religious homogeneity. It is derived from percentage differences arising from six different religious groupings, Catholic, Protestant, Buddhist, Hindu, Moslem, and Jewish. The calculation procedure is essentially the same as for dyadic language homogeneity.

11. In each of these three countries, at least one indigenous polling agency was contacted to determine if similar questions had been asked over a twelve-year period. In each instance, no relevant questions were asked periodically over that interval.
12. A discussion of the use of different questions over time to measure the same attitude appears in Pool, Abelson, and Popkin (1965).

The third submeasure relates to racial homogeneity and is based on percentage differences in the racial distribution in the populations of two nations (i.e., percent Negro, percent Caucasian, and percent Mongolian). The measurement procedure is again the same as for language homogeneity.

The overall measure of cultural homogeneity is formed through an optimally weighted combination of these three submeasures. As to data, the primary source on the distribution of languages was the *United Nations Demographic Yearbook*, while religious and racial distributions were obtained from DON.

COMMON HISTORICAL ATTRIBUTES

Several variables are used to measure the extent to which two nations possess comparable historical attributes. The first is relative age as a recognizable political unit. Age is based on a five-point scale, taken from DON, indicating the date at which a country came to possess an internationally recognizable border and some form of central administration (Rummel, 1964). The second variable relates to the possession of colonies. A dyad is recognized as homogeneous if either or both of its member nations possessed colonies, the measure being derived from monadic DON data. The third historical variable is the relative stability of the two governmental systems represented in a dyad. Governmental stability is defined in terms of a four-point scale, taken from Banks and Textor. The stability measure ranges from general, overall stability predating World War I to general instability dating from World War II. The influence of common historical attributes in the global system will be assessed through the use of a weighted function of these three variables.

In the regional study, the indicator of common historical experience is alignment during World War II. All North Atlantic dyads are classified according to one of three categories: allies, neutrals, or opponents. Allies are those in the same alignment such as the United States–Great Britain or Germany–Italy. Neutral dyads are those including at least one member not taking an officially declared part in the war, for example, all dyads including Switzerland. Opponents refer to antagonistic dyads such as the United States–Germany.

HOMOGENEITY OF SOCIAL WELFARE AND DYADIC WELFARE DENSITY

Social welfare will be defined here in terms of three welfare values: (1) health—persons per physician, (2) education—primary school pupils as a portion of the primary-school-age population, and   (3) employment (reflected)—number of unemployed as a percent of the working-age population. Data on all three of these variables comes primarily from the DON project. Weighted measures of homogeneity with respect to these variables are used to index dyadic homogeneity of social welfare, and weighted mean values are taken collectively to measure dyadic welfare density.

HOMOGENEITY OF DEVELOPMENT AND DEVELOPMENTAL DENSITY

Four variables commonly cited by students of modernity as indicators of a nation's socioeconomic development provide the basis for our dyadic measures of developmental homogeneity and density. They are (1) industrialization (reflected)—the percentage of a nation's population depending directly upon agriculture for their livelihood,   (2) urbanization—the percentage of the population living in cities of 20,000 or more, (3) literacy (reflected)—the percentage of the adult population which is illiterate, and   (4) per capita wealth—the national income per capita. The major source of data for all four of these variables was again the DON project. Weighted measures of homogeneity with respect to these variables are taken as indicators of developmental homogeneity, and weighted measures are used to represent dyadic developmental density.

COMMON REGIME STABILITY AND AVERAGE LENGTH OF POLITICAL REGIME

The average tenure of the last two executive heads of government as of 1955 (DON) is used to measure the stability of a nation's political regime. Again both a dyadic homogeneity measure and a dyadic mean value of this variable are calculated for use in the study.

HOMOGENEITY OF MILITARY POWER AND ITS AVERAGE MAGNITUDE

The military power of a nation is measured by its total defense expenditure (in American dollars) and by its total military personnel. Both are derived from the DON data with inductively weighted measures of homogeneity based on dyadic ratios of these two variables. Dyadic means, appropriately weighted, are taken as indicators of the overall military strength of the nation-pair.

HOMOGENEITY AND AVERAGE LEVEL
OF ECONOMIC POWER

Relative and mean measures of gross national product (GNP) and energy potential, both based primarily on DON data, are used as indicators of the commonality and level of economic power in a dyad. The first variable, GNP, is assumed to measure a nation's realized economic power, while energy potential is taken to be representative of the economic resources that the nation can ultimately draw upon. Composite measures of dyadic homogeneity and average level of economic power are again formed through the assignment of inductively derived weightings of the respective submeasures.

HOMOGENEITY AND AVERAGE LEVEL
OF BUREAUCRATIC DEVELOPMENT

Measures of the commonality and average level of bureaucratic development are based on Banks and Textor's fourfold classification of "average character of the bureaucracy." The four-point scale ranges from "modern generally effective and responsible civil service" to "traditional large non-rationalized bureaucratic structure."

(3) Background Factors: Systemic Properties The final set of background factors to be operationally defined concerns systemic properties. These are inherently nonmonadic characteristics of nation-sets. Here we are specifically interested in dyadic indicators of past patterns of international collaboration.

The previous collaborative experience of two nations will be measured by the scope and frequency of formal intergovernmental treaty arrangements dating from 1815 to 1952 for the regional study and from 1815 to 1955 for the global study. A formal intergovernmental treaty arrangement is defined as a treaty, convention, protocol, agreement, or exchange of notes recognized and recorded by the United Nations or its precursors. According to Starke, a treaty applies to a more serious political contract; a convention is of more limited scope and signed with less formalized ritual; a protocol, or an agreement, is less formal than either of the above and is never in "heads of state form."[13] Finally, he notes, an

13. This means that the specific leaders of nations such as President or Prime Minister are never explicitly mentioned in the text.

exchange of notes is the most informal when there is no document, but states merely inform other states that certain actions will be recognized as binding upon them. Multilateral arrangements are treated as distinct arrangements between all possible dyadic combinations of the participating nations.

For our purposes no distinction of salience will be made among treaties, conventions, protocols, agreements, and exchanges of notes. According to Starke, each involves either subscriptions to certain understandings or recognition of certain binding obligations. As he suggests, the type of contract or legal instrument is here considered less important than the substantive area of agreement.

Collaborative arrangements of nine substantive types are considered: (1) political, (2) military, (3) trade, (4) economic, (5) legal, (6) transportation, (7) cultural, (8) technical and scientific, and (9) other.[14] Weighted frequencies of agreements in these nine areas are taken collectively to define the scope and intensity of previous collaborative experience.

(4) Mutual Relevance   The model we have outlined is predicated on the assumption that the mutual relevance of two nations is established behaviorally through the intensity and extensity of intercourse between them. More specifically, mutual relevance is defined in terms of various forms of nongovernmental contact between persons in one nation and those in another. Operationally, a linear additive function of the relative frequency of contact between two nations along eight ranges of interaction will be taken as a measure of their mutual relevance. An attempt was made to obtain data on a variety of indicators, particularly those mentioned by Deutsch (1962, 212–218) as essential in measuring cooperation as a measure of "responsiveness."

The eight variables utilized are   (1) mail (letters and postcards),

---

14. Some examples of typical coding entries under each heading are included here. Most pacts classified as political were amity pacts. Those listed as military included mutual assistance pacts and exchanges of military armaments. Trade pacts included agreements regarding exchanges of goods. Economic pacts included loans or aid. Legal arrangements included settlement of property claims and extradition agreements. Transportation pacts referred to regulation of waterways and airline agreements. Cultural pacts referred to exchange of ballet groups, art objects, etc. Technical pacts concerned peaceful uses of atomic energy and space research. Other was a residual category and included only a small number of items like establishment of wildlife stations.

(2) telegraph (telegrams), (3) telephone (calls), (4) telex (radio-grams), (5) trade (in American dollars), (6) student-teacher exchange (persons), (7) tourism (overnight visitors traveling for business or pleasure), and (8) common nongovernmental memberships (NGO) in the same international nongovernmental organizations.[15] In accord with Jacob and Teune's threefold typology of transactional variables, the first four are measures of dyadic communication of the interchange of messages. The fifth, trade, represents the exchange of goods and services, while the last three variables correspond to what Jacob and Teune term "mobility" and are measures of the movement of persons and/or the frequency of personal contact.

Each of these eight measures of inter-nation contact is seen as contributing to mutual relevance in terms of the relative proportion it represents of the total contact of its kind which the members of a given dyad have with all nations under study. In other words, the mutual relevance indicated by any one variable is a function of the amount of mutual attention shown through it by two nations in comparison to the total attention of that variety displayed by those two nations. Thus, the importance assigned to a unit of contact between two nations is anchored in the patterns of international behavior peculiar to those nations.

Data acquisition for the eight variables defining "mutual relevance" proved to be the most problematic of our data collection activities. Because of this, brief attention to each is in order.

Mail. The primary source for mail flow data (i.e., letters and postcards) is the *Statistique des Expeditions dans L'Service Postal International*, a triennial publication of the Universal Postal Union since 1922. The major problem with this source is that several nations, including the United States and Canada, did not provide such data for the Universal Postal Union (UPU). In addition, the UPU discontinued the publication of these statistics with the 1961 edition. To fill the gaps, letters were sent to national postal ministries requesting mail flow data or estimates thereof for the year 1955 in the global study. Similar requests were made to the postal ministries of the North Atlantic countries for 1964 and they all responded.

In the global study, many nations did not keep records of the exact number of letters and postcards sent to other countries, but all provided

15. All of the above measures were used in the global study. Two were not included in the regional study. Telephone calls were not included since there was no way to estimate numbers in a directional sense; and estimation procedures had to be used for telex and telegram calls. NGO membership was not used since all members in the North Atlantic region were the most active NGO participants of all nations in the world. This was no variation on this indicator.

information from which estimates could be made. Generally, this is in the form of the total weight (either in grams or pounds) of first-class surface and/or air mail going to various countries. The postal variable is restricted to letters and postcards, since many post offices, including those of the United States and Canada, do not keep information dyadically on any other form of postal exchange.

Telegraph-Telephone-Telex.   Estimates of the number of telegrams, telephone calls, and radiograms interchanged between nations in 1955 are obtained from statistics published by the International Telecommunications Union (ITU) (viz., *The Telecommunications Journal, The General Plan for the Development of the International Network, General Telegram Statistics, General Telephone Statistics,* and *Telex Statistics*). Because 1957 was the first year that the ITU kept data on the inter-nation flow of telex data, 1955 estimates are obtained by extrapolating these data to 1955 totals. All three forms of telecommunications are restricted to private persons and organizations exclusive of the government.[16]

Trade.   Data on inter-nation trade is obtained from the publications of the United Nations and the International Monetary Fund.[17] Because the import-export records of any two nations tend to vary somewhat, the average of the total trade within the dyad is used to characterize both directional and summed dyads.

Student-Teacher Exchange.   Information on the number of students and teachers exchanged between countries is obtained from publications of the United Nations Educational, Scientific, and Cultural Organization.[18]

Tourism.   Information on tourist travel is kept by the International Union of Official Travel Organizations (IUOTO) and is published annually in *International Travel Statistics.* Unfortunately, nations are not consistent in the type of data they report. Thus, the statistics published by the IUOTO may be on the number of foreign visitors entering a country and/or the number of tourist-nights spent in a country by visitors from other nations. In order to have comparable data for all countries, statistics of the latter variety are used to obtain estimates of the number of actual tourists from different countries.

Common NGO Memberships.   The tenth edition of the *Yearbook of International Organizations* is the source of membership data. Fortunately, the information has been recorded on punch cards by the Peace

16. Some countries do not keep statistics on the amount of governmental exchanges, hence this information was not included.
17. For references, see the Bibliography under "Data Sources."
18. For references, see the Bibliography under "Data Sources."

Research Institute in Oslo, Norway, and we were able to obtain the information through the offices of P. Smoker, Research Associate, Simulated International Project, Northwestern University, and the Peace Research Centre, Lancaster, England.

(5) *Inter-*   The last component of the model for the study
governmental   of inter-nation collaboration is intergovern-
Collaboration   mental interaction. Like previous collaborative experience, formal collaboration is defined operationally in terms of the number of treaty arrangements of various substantive types between two nations. All agreements involving dyadic combinations of the forty-nine nations under study recorded by the United Nations in its *Treaty Series, Cumulative Index* for the period since 1815 are included. In the regional study, pacts signed between 1815–1952 are classified as "past integrative experience." After 1952, such collaborative efforts are treated as current intergovernmental cooperation. In the global study, the dividing line is 1955. Prior and up to that year is regarded as "previous collaboration," the period from 1956–1958 is regarded as current collaboration. Material for these periods are divided into the same substantive categories used for previous collaborative experience, and multilateral arrangements are again treated in terms of dyadic combinations of the nations involved.[19]

Missing Data   Data availability is a primary consideration in the selection of observations for study. While this tends to reduce the problems of missing data, the concern was not completely eliminated. There are, of course, several standard procedures for handling missing data. Among the most common of these is the practice of substituting some measure of central tendency, such as a mean, for the missing datum. Rather than resort to such procedures, however, more realistic estimates are made through interpolation or extrapolation of available data.

In terms of unit, or societal, properties this meant scouring through the sources of data on the relevant variables to find observations on measures as proximate to the year desired as possible. If sufficient cross-temporal data could be found to assess a trend (i.e., for three or more time-periods), this is taken into account in the estimate; otherwise, the

19. The classification scheme employed in this study is similar to that of Rohn (1966), who formulated a more elaborate scheme.

nearest temporal value of the variable is considered as an estimate of the missing datum.

With respect to interaction variables, the procedures used to cope with missing data are similar. While we have either global or regional measures of total interaction for all nations in the study, the problem centers on filling the missing cells in a matrix of dyadic relationships. An effort was first made to find a value for that cell in a similar matrix of data as temporally proximate to the year desired as possible. The proportion of the marginal total represented by that cell in the new matrix was then determined and a like proportion of the desired year's total assigned to the missing cell in the original matrix. If a value could not be found for a missing cell in any subsequent or preceding matrix of like data, the value assigned to the original cell was determined by the mean proportion represented by that relational cell in the matrix for the other interaction variables included in the study. The sole restriction imposed on these estimates was that their sum for any nation not exceed that portion of its total after all identified dyadic relationships had been taken out. If necessary to meet this restriction, the estimates were proportionally pared.

Selection of Different approaches to analyzing time inter-
Time Intervals vals were taken in the regional and global
studies. In the global system only one time-in-
terval was selected in order to develop a composite picture of a partial international system at one point in time. A cross-sectional time-lag study focusing on the year 1955 was selected primarily because of data availability on a variety of measures. In addition, a cross-sectional approach is more appropriate when there is a paucity of research in the area (M. Haas, 117). The lack of systematic research efforts to determine the precursors of international collaboration reinforced the decision to employ a cross-sectional design. As M. Haas has written,

> There is considerable empirical similarity between the results of both kinds of analysis (i.e., longitudinal and cross-sectional). With only a few exceptions the conclusions of longitudinal analysis have been identical with those of cross-sectional analysis . . . the additional theoretical payoff from the former may not be worth the extra labor when one is trying to build theory in a previously unexplored field [117].

In the regional area, there are a great many empirical studies, but most are cross-sectional in focus. M. Haas (117), however, has written that longitudinal analysis may be the most appropriate in study communities where there have been a number of case studies, as is true in the North Atlantic area. Thus, different time-approaches are relevant when the state of the literature varies as is the case in regional and global studies of community formation.

In the study of the North Atlantic region, a key consideration is that a number of indicators such as attitudes and transactions, particularly mail exchange, were not available on a yearly basis for a large sample. As a result, a three-year interval was chosen over a twelve-year period. The year 1952 was selected as the beginning point, since there was a paucity of attitudinal information prior to that time. With a two-year lag in publication of data sources, 1964 was selected as the point of termination. Between 1952–1964, this would allow five time-cuts for analysis: 1952, 1955, 1958, 1961, and 1964.[20] A three-year interval was chosen because, on the average, there were no more than five opinion samplings on most questions during this interval. Secondly, a three-year lag was present for many of the transactional indicators such as mail. Data on student exchange and tourism was not complete on an annual basis, but using the three-year interval eliminated the problem of missing data or data estimation for several variables. Thirdly, many of the theorists' notions discussed previously such as those of Deutsch occurred over a longer period of time, from several years to a decade or more. In this instance, the need to have yearly time-intervals was not a primary desire. All information was recorded for relevant years except telex information, which was not gathered in 1952. One other exception was noted for intergovernmental collaboration. Four intervals were examined: 1952–1954, 1955–1957, 1958–1960 and 1961–1963. The data for 1964–1966 was not yet available when the study was completed.

Techniques for Data Analysis   The techniques used for analyzing transactional data are varied; however, the repetitiveness in the use of a particular form of analysis requires a brief comment.

Relative Acceptance Indices.   The prevailing form of analysis employed in examining transaction flows is the Relative Acceptance (RA) index. This is a modified chi square technique used to compute measures of relative acceptance from dyadic transaction data (Deutsch and Sav-

20. In some instances, the attitude sampling did not correspond with the year. To achieve uniformity, a measure taken within three months of the desired year was classified under that year. For example, October–December, 1954, would be included under 1955 if there were a relevant opinion sampling in that period and no sampling during 1955 for the same dyad.

age).[21] Although the authors of such studies generally argue from a communications point-of-view (Brams, 1966, 1967; Russett, 1963), the implicit logic of the procedure is more consistent with field theory, as discussed in Chapter 1. Brams (1966), for example, contends that the RA index provides measures of the "effective distance" which separate two social entities. He reasons that this distance may be considered an aggregate measure of "component factors such as geographical proximity, ideological compatibility and cultural homogeneity" (883). These assertions resemble theoretic field notions.

Although the assumptions underlying the RA measure may find justification in either communications or field theory, the procedure itself creates an interesting, albeit familiar, conceptual problem. Namely, is the index a measure of a cause or an effect? That is, is it an indicator of attribute distance or is the behavior an effect of attribute distance? The issue may be, and has been, avoided by using RAs simply to describe a system at a given point in time or to describe trends in a system over time. But the issue cannot be so easily blurred if explanatory propositions are sought. To understand the relationship between background attributes and behavior requires distinct measures of both. Inglehart (1968) highlights the problems as follows:

> It [the RA index] does not indicate whether given political effects are likely to occur. For this purpose, a simple measure of the relative size of the transaction may be more appropriate [122].[22]

Canonical Correlation Analysis. Given the analytic demands of the study as previously outlined, we felt that the RA technique would be inadequate. In terms of method, the study demands a procedure for analyzing a multiplicity of variables simultaneously, while at the same time preserving the identity, or integrity, of each. Further, the problems posed for analysis require a method for treating not only a number of predictors at one time but a number of criterion variables at the same

21. The relative acceptance (RA_{ij}) of a nation j for a nation i is defined as the difference between the observed or actual exchange (A_{ij}) and a hypothetically expected exchange value (E_{ij}) divided by the expected exchange:

$$RA_{ij} = \frac{A_{ij} - E_{ij}}{E_{ij}}, \text{ where } -1 < RA_{ij} < \infty$$

The expected exchange (E_{ij}) is derived from marginal totals in an exchange matrix on the assumption of indifference (i.e., origin destination independence). Because the diagonal cells ($i = j$) in an exchange matrix are zero cells, the standard chi square procedures for obtaining expected values are not strictly applicable. Rather, a series of successive approximations are employed to obtain the expected exchange. See Goodman (1964).

22. All canonical solutions in the following three chapters are based on relative magnitudes of variables rather than absolute magnitudes.

time. To meet these needs, we used two multivariate correlational methods, canonical correlational analysis and multiple regression. Most are probably familiar with the latter mode of analysis, but not with the first.

Canonical correlational analysis is a statistical technique that may be used to determine the maximum correlation between two sets of variables. For example, suppose we have p predictors and q criteria; the problem is to find sets of weightings that will allow the most criteria variance to be explained by the predictors. In other words, we want to find the sets of weightings, or if you like, the regression coefficients that will maximize the correlation between the p predictors and q criteria. Canonical analysis enables us to find such optimally weighted linear additive functions of the p predictors and q criteria. For the special case where q or $p = 1$, the problem is simply one of multiple regression. If both p and $q = 1$, we have a simple case of bivariate, or product-moment, correlation.

Thus, canonical analysis may be considered a generalized form of the commonplace bivariate, or product-moment, form of correlation analysis. In fact, canonical correlations are identical to simple bivariate correlations between the derived canonical variates, (i.e., the weighted functions of the p and q variables). In the bivariate case, the strength of a correlation is determined by finding the best possible "fit" in the sense of reducing to a minimum the sum of squares of the discrepancies about a regression line. Similarly, the multivariate procedures used here are designed to find the p and q dimensional planes, or hyperplanes, with the best possible correspondence in $p + q$ dimensional space. "Best" is used in the sense of producing the least sum of squared discrepancies.

Although the statistical theory underlying canonical correlation and regression is essentially the same as that for the bivariate case, the mathematics involved are considerably more complicated. For a detailed discussion of the theory and mathematics involved in canonical analysis, the reader is referred to Anderson, Cooley, and Lohnes; McKeon, and Rao.

Whereas bivariate analysis yields a unique solution, canonical correlational analysis yields a unique set of solutions. In fact, there will be m nonzero orthogonal (independent) solutions where m equals less than either p or q. A solution consists of an eigenvalue, or latent root, and an associated eigenvector. The eigenvalue represents the squared canonical correlation between the p predictors and q criteria when these are weighted in accord with the respective weightings contained in the associated eigenvector. The square root of the first eigenvalue represents the maximum canonical correlation, and the associated eigenvector provides the most predictable criterion weightings (i.e., the optimal weightings for standardized measures of the $p + q$ variables).

The comparative advantages of canonical analysis are several. First, in a purely statistical sense, one is much more likely to meet the assumptions of normality in multivariate, or composite, measures than in single variable measures. This is a demonstrable consequence of the well-known Central Limit Theorem.[23] Secondly, the technique allows us to assay the relationship between sets or systems of variables without having to assume the quantitative equivalence of all variables within a set. In other words, a number of variables may be included in an analysis without destroying their identity or their internal pattern within a set. Thirdly, through the assignment of canonical weightings to standardized measures of the variables in each set, canonical analysis allows us to assess the relative contribution or importance of each variable in the set. Because of this, indices of concepts manifested or indicated through a number of behavioral measures can be constructed inductively using best-predictor weightings rather than some arbitrary a priori procedure. Finally, canonical analysis is subject to relatively straightforward interpretations. Like its bivariate counterpart, canonical analysis measures common variance which when squared indicates the percentage of criteria variance explained by the predictors. Unlike the Pearson product-moment correlation which may range from -1 to $+1$, canonical correlations to include multiple R may vary from zero to $+1$, zero indicating no relationship and 1 indicating a perfect predictor-criterion relationship.[24]

For all of these reasons, canonical correlational analysis seems well suited to the demands of the present study. The canonical solutions presented in the next chapter were obtained using the BMD 06 computer program on Northwestern University's CDC 3400 computer. The calculation procedures entail partitioning a matrix of bivariate correlations into four submatrices of inter- and intra-predictor and criterion correlations. These were then used to solve the matrix equations, which yielded the desired eigenvalues and eigenvectors (i.e., the squared canonical correlations and their associated variable weightings). All of the weighting coefficients that are presented are based on standardized measures of the variables involved and are thus directly comparable.[25]

In presenting canonical solutions, the maximum correlation (RC_{max}) and its corresponding variable weightings will be given. Of the remaining $q-1$ or $p-1$ canonical solutions, we will report solutions only when their magnitude approximates that of the maximum solution. The statistics we report are considered summary descriptive measures, but under the inferential assumptions of the product-moment correlation and with

23. For a demonstration of the formal proof, see Anderson et al. (74–79, 288–305).
24. The direction of a relationship can be determined by an inspection of the signs of the regression coefficients.
25. This is a direct consequence of the canonical technique.

1176 observations, a *r* of .06 or more would be significant at the .05 level. In the North Atlantic study, correlations of .271 and .135 would be significant for the 52 and 210 dyads respectively.[26] Under like assumptions, any canonical correlation contained within the global study greater than .16 would be significant at the .05 level, while a solution in the North Atlantic area greater than .44 would be significant.

Conclusion In this chapter, we have outlined the general research strategy used to investigate empirically the hypothesis posited in Chapter 3. The objective is to link background variables to patterns of mutual relevance. These patterns, in turn, are used as predictors of the scope and frequency of formal collaboration represented by the number of various substantive types of intergovernmental arrangements in subsequent three-year periods. To accomplish this objective, two research designs have been discussed, one for a global and one for a regional perspective. The procedures and rationales for such a dualistic approach also have been discussed. The observations used to explore these hypotheses consist of 1176 dyadic combinations of forty-nine nations in the year 1955 for the global study and 210 combinations of fifteen nations observed at five different points in time from 1952–1964 for the regional study. Operational definitions have been discussed and the sources from whence the necessary data were obtained have been identified. Finally, we have discussed the statistical procedures used in analyzing these sets of data. We are now prepared to consider the results of that analysis in the next three chapters.

26. When attitudinal variables are involved, 52 dyads are included; when attitudes are not involved, 210 dyads constitute the sample.

PART III

EMPIRICAL
FINDINGS

chapter 5

Mutual Relevance and the Impact of Geophysical Properties

Introduction   In reporting the results of our empirical investigation we will use the same general format employed in Chapter 3. Consideration will be given first to the preliminary hypothesis regarding the interrelationships among the various indicators of mutual relevance. Attention will then be directed to the hypotheses linking the three types of background factors to mutual relevance. Finally, the relationship between mutual relevance and intergovernmental collaboration will be explored. The results which will be presented are, of course, subject to the limitations of our data and operational definitions. For ease of presentation and to spare the reader the tedium of repetition of these reservations, we will adopt a somewhat didactic style. Nonetheless, the qualified nature of our findings must be borne in mind.

Interrelationships   Consonant with a general assumption found
Among Indicators of   in the literature on international relations, we
Mutual Relevance   have hypothesized a positive relationship among various measures of transnational intercourse. In the regional study, the interrelationship among the various forms of transactional exchange can be examined at various intervals.

The correlation matrix for the various interaction measures in 1952 and the correlations between transactions in 1952 and 1964 are presented in Table 5.1.[1]

Proposition 1 is confirmed in the North Atlantic area, as all correlations are .4 or higher with particularly high correlations among mail and other transactional indicators. Transactions are highly congruent at one point in time and over time as well. The lowest set of correlations is linked with student exchange, particularly tourism, which tends to indicate that information flows (mail, telegraph) are more highly interrelated than exchange of goods.[2]

In the global study, Proposition 1 is also substantially borne out for the eight indicators used in the present study. As can be seen from Table 5.2, the upper half of the matrix shown in the table contains the intercorrelations among absolute measures of the various interaction variables. While these correlations are only of incidental interest to the present study, they do show that there is a positive relationship among the various forms of international interaction, but in no case are the relationships

TABLE 5.1

Correlation Matrix for Transactions in 1952 and 1952–1964

	MAIL	STUD	TELG	TOUR	TRAD
Mail					
Stud	.68 (.70)				
Telg	.80 (.81)	.46 (.40)			
Tour	.68 (.72)	.40 (.43)	.65 (.60)		
Trad	.80 (.82)	.54 (.50)	.76 (.79)	.46 (.41)	

The correlations for 1952 are presented first, those for 1952–1964 are presented in parentheses.

1. Telex data was not collected until 1957 and was not included in the above matrix. The correlations for 1955, 1958, 1961, and 1964 were of roughly equal magnitudes for all variables; see Cobb (1967, Appendix 4, Tables 1 and 2). All correlations were computed on the CDC 3400 computer with the BMD 03D program. All correlations are significant at the .05 level.
2. There is sufficient variation in correlations among indicators to suggest some independence and to continue use of the group of variables rather than choosing one as a representative for the set of transactions. When using a canonical program to predict from 1952 transactions to 1964 transactions, a solution of .99 was obtained, with mail having the highest loading; see Cobb (1967, Appendix 4, Table 3) for the solution.

TABLE 5.2

Correlations Among Eight Relative and Absolute Indicators of Dyadic Intercourse between Nations in 1955

	MAIL	TELG	TELP	TELX	TRAD	STUD	TOUR	NGO
Mail	(.81)	.66	.78	.28	.82	.69	.78	.36
Telegraph	.64	(.65)	.67	.11	.70	.68	.67	.22
Telephone	.70	.59	(.77)	.25	.82	.70	.90	.28
Telex	.26	.35	.35	(.70)	.24	.22	.22	.41
Trade	.57	.53	.63	.42	(.90)	.81	.77	.35
Student Exchange	.48	.45	.49	.42	.63	(.81)	.67	.28
Tourism	.49	.48	.65	.29	.45	.39	(.67)	.35
Common NGOs	.30	.34	.30	.43	.44	.34	.29	(.96)

The upper half of the matrix represents the correlations among absolute measures of inter-nation interaction. The lower half of the matrix contains the correlations among relative measures of these same forms of interaction. The diagonal elements show the correlation between the absolute and relative measures.

substantial enough to indicate that any one measure could serve adequately to represent all.

Of more immediate interest are the correlations in the lower half of the matrix. These represent the relationships among the relative measures which serve as indicators of mutual relevance. The conclusion we draw from these correlations is essentially the same as for the absolute measures. While the measures show a positive relational tendency, they are by no means congruent.

It will be observed that the correlations among the absolute measures tend to be somewhat larger than those among the relative measures. As a correlation coefficient is quite sensitive to the extremes in a distribution, this result may be viewed largely as an artifact of a few highly internationally active and inactive nations. By grounding dyadic intercourse in the patterns of international behavior exhibited by the nations involved, this exaggeration effect is removed. As might then be expected, the correlations among the relative measures are more homogeneous.

In way of general conclusions, while there is a positive interrelationship among the various forms of international intercourse, the link is much less substantial than is commonly supposed. We take these results as confirmation of Deutsch's frequent assertion of the necessity to consider multiple transactions when attempting to assess the mutual relevance of two nations.

The Linkage
Between
Geophysical
Properties and
Mutual Relevance

We have offered hypotheses linking three types of background factors to patterns of mutual relevance. These include (1) properties of the geophysical environment; (2) unit, or societal, properties; and (3) systemic properties. With regard to almost all of the factors contained within these three sets, we found disparate assessments of their influence on international behavior. These competing strands of thought are mirrored in the hypotheses which we will now attempt to evaluate empirically. Geophysical properties presumably influence patterns of mutual relevance through the material and psychic costs of involvement they represent. Of particular interest is the concept of geographic proximity.

Geographic Proximity. In the regional study, the relationship between proximity and attitudinal components was studied as well as the linkage with transactional indicators. The linkage between proximity and resultant attitudes which has been posited assumes that propinquity will lead to mutual awareness and understanding (Buchanan and Cantril, 38–44). In correlating proximity with attitudinal distributions in 1952, a figure of —.24 is obtained for the affective component and a correlation of —.09 for the policy component.[3] Furthermore, in examining the relationship between common boundaries and mass perceptions in 1952, the correlation for the affective component is —.27 and —.05 for the policy component.[4] Proposition 2b is supported, as there is no strong tie between proximity and the affective component, nor is proximity linked strongly with attitudes toward regional unity.

In examining the relationship between proximity and transactional exchange, an absence of a strong tie is also found by examining the correlation matrix in Table 5.3.

The only correlations of any magnitude involved the linkage of common boundaries and mail exchange and trade.[5] Clearly there is not

---

3. The correlations for other attitudinal distributions in 1955, 1958, 1961, and 1964 were of similar magnitude and can be found in Cobb (1967, Appendix 4). Neither correlation set is significant at the .05 level.

4. Neither correlation is significant at the .05 level. A similar pattern exists at other time-intervals; see Cobb (1967, Appendix 4) for the correlations.

5. None of the above correlations is significant at the .05 level. None of the findings was of any larger magnitude for other years. See Cobb (1967, Appendix 4, Table 7) for the correlations.

TABLE 5.3

*The Relationship Between Common Boundaries, Proximity, and
Transactional Exchange in 1952*

	COMMON BOUNDARIES	PROXIMITY
Mail	.13	.16
Stud	.15	.04
Telg	.03	.10
Tour	.01	.10
Trad	.14	.20

a clear propensity to interact with other nations solely because they are more proximate than other states or share a common boundary. The importance of geographic proximity as an overriding determinant in explaining transactional exchange has been overplayed.

In the global study, the pattern is not the same. The results presented in Table 5.4 are generally supportive of the link between proximity and interaction (Proposition 2a). There is a distinct tendency for geographically more proximate nations to exhibit greater mutual relevance. It is particularly interesting to note the importance of territorial contiguity. Proximity has its greatest influence through the sharing of a common boundary. Not surprisingly, its influence on mutual relevance is most markedly found in tourist travel.

Although the effect is much less pronounced (Rc .26 as opposed to the Rc_{max} of .57), the second canonical solution suggests that noncontiguous proximity may have a somewhat different effect on mutual relevance. Although it is a clearly subordinate pattern, mail, trade, and even tourism tend to be somewhat greater between remote nations than between more proximate but noncontiguous ones. Telegraph communications, student exchange, and common NGO memberships, on the other hand, tend to be greater between more proximate though noncontiguous nations.

The primary conclusion we would draw, however, is based on the dominant relational tendency indicated in the first canonical solution: proximity tends to have a positive influence on the mutual relevance of two nations. The lack of salience in the North Atlantic community may be attributed to the key role of its remoter member, the United States, and the relatively restricted variance resulting from a contained geographical area. However, in the larger study, the salience of proximity cannot be denied.

TABLE 5.4

Geographical Proximity as a Predictor of Mutual Relevance

BIVARIATE CORRELATIONS

Inter-Predictor: Common Boundary
  Geographical Distance $-.28$
Predictor-Criterion

	Mail	Telg	Telp	Telx	Trad	Stud	Tour	NGO
Geo Dist	$-.20$	$-.28$	$-.24$	$-.25$	$-.28$	$-.21$	$-.20$	$-.32$
Com Bound	.41	.33	.44	.30	.33	.29	.48	.21

CANONICAL SOLUTIONS

First Solution: $Rc_{max} = .57$

Predictor Weightings[a]			Criterion Weightings[a]			
Geo Dist	Com Bound	Mail	Telg	Telp	Telx	
$-.39$	$+.82$	.26	.06	.09	.26	
			Trad	Stud	Tour	NGO
			$-.08$	.06	.56	.13

Second Solution: $Rc_2 = .26$

Predictor Weightings[a]			Criterion Weightings[a]			
Geo Dist	Com Bound	Mail	Telg	Telp	Telx	
$-.97$	$-.65$	$-.61$	.62	$-.06$	$-.06$	
			Trad	Stud	Tour	NGO
			$-.49$	.36	$-.26$	.85

[a] Coefficients are for standardized measures.

chapter 6

Unit Properties
and Mutual Relevance

Introduction   The internal traits of nations themselves may
be seen as wellsprings of international be-
havior. We have identified a number of societal properties which are
presumably relevant to the course of international interaction and have
offered hypotheses specifying the nature of these linkages. Again disparate threads of discourse were found regarding the transactional influence of most of these factors, and recourse sought through empirical
analysis.

Belief Systems and   The first societal trait to be investigated in-
System Practices: volves the dynamics of belief systems encom-
Homogeneity of   passing key values and salient attitudes.
Major Political   Values are defined in two different ways: the
Values   existence of certain practices or institutional
forms, and the persistence of certain salient
attitudes distributed among the mass population. The first will be exam-
ined in a global system, since there would be little differentiation in the
North Atlantic region with regard to the specific values examined. Attitudinal dimensions will be examined in a regional context.

The prevailing assumption in the literature seems to be that the
more homogeneous two nations in terms of operative political values, the

greater the relative interaction between them. This is based on the pre-sumption that common values tend to foster common identifications and interests. We were able to find exception to this assumption and, there-fore, entertained both the proposition asserting the linkage between homogeneity and interaction and its null counterpart.

Because of the importance generally attached to the sharing of political values by students of international relations, we found the results presented in Table 6.1 rather startling. While there is evidence of a relationship in the predicted direction (Proposition 3a), it is hardly substantial. Frankly, we had expected a much stronger relationship to be evinced between value homogeneity and mutual relevance. As can be seen from the first canonical solution, what effect the sharing of political values does have on patterns of mutual relevance is manifested largely through common membership in NGOs. Shared political values seem to have little or no influence on any other form of transnational intercourse.

We are obliged to accept the proposition (3a) that value homo-geneity does influence mutual relevance. But the far more interesting find-

TABLE 6.1

Political Value Homogeneity as a Predictor of Mutual Relevance

BIVARIATE CORRELATIONS			
Inter-Predictor:	Free Op	Press Cens	Comm Part
Free Opposition	1.00	.59	.05
Press Censorship	.59	1.00	.07
Communist Party	.05	.07	1.00

Predictor-Criterion:								
	Mail	Telg	Telp	Telx	Trad	Stud	Tour	NGO
Free Op	.09	.09	.08	.12	.14	.11	.07	.21
Press Cens	.10	.12	.13	.17	.18	.13	.11	.30
Comm Part	.05	.01	.08	.06	.07	.07	.03	.09

CANONICAL SOLUTIONS

First Solution: $Rc_{max} = .32$

Predictor Weightings[a]			Criterion Weightings[a]			
Free Op	Press Cens	Comm Part	Mail	Telg	Telp	Telx
.12	.87	.24	−.14	−.01	.20	.10
			Trad	Stud	Tour	NGO
			.12	0.3	−.05	.86

Second Solution: $Rc_2 = .08$
Third Solution: $Rc_3 = .06$

[a] Coefficients are for standardized measures.

ing is the relatively minor role shared values play in inter-nation interaction. This finding leads us to doubt that the essence of international cooperation lies in shared political values, as alleged.

Belief Systems and System Practices: The Salience of Certain Key Attitudes   An alternative means of examining values is to investigate the nature of certain attitudinal clusters among mass publics as well as studying the "open-ness" of a system. In the North Atlantic study, mass opinion was considered to be a key determinant of the cohesiveness of a region.

Linkage Between Affective and Policy Components. A high correlation between the affective and policy components of mass attitudes has been posited (Proposition 4a). In the North Atlantic area with a total of fifty-two directional dyads over a twelve-year span from 1952–1964, the product-moment correlation between the affective and policy components is .10.[1] This indicates that Proposition 4b is supported on an aggregate level, as various aspects of mass opinion are not related. Masses which perceive other nations favorably do not necessarily endorse policies favoring regional integration. Each aspect must be treated separately in ensuing analysis.

Stability of Attitudes. Mass opinion has been characterized as "moody" in foreign policy deliberations in which over time there are frequent and sharp upward and downward swings evincing no popular commitment to a particular viewpoint (Almond, 54). Yet others argue that opinions are stable (Key, 256–257). In this instance, the stability of the policy and policy components can be studied.

One way to determine opinion stability is to take the opinion distribution at each of the five points in time and correlate each time-period (e.g., 1952) with the other four and take the average Pearson correlation for the time periods to determine the amount of divergence.[2] For the affective component the average correlation is .91, while the correlation is only .65 for the policy component during the same periods.

In gauging stability, the standard error of estimate can also be computed to determine the extent to which opinion responses vary from

1. This correlation is not significant at the .05 level. In this chapter, correlations are used for descriptive rather than inferential purposes. But arbitrary cut-off points (i.e., significance levels) are used for purposes of evaluation.
2. With five time-intervals, this would mean ten correlations covering the following time-periods: 1952–1955, 1952–1958, 1952–1961, 1952–1964, 1955–1958, 1955–1961, 1955–1964, 1958–1961, 1958–1964, and 1961–1964.

the regression line.[3] The attitude measures can vary from 0 to 100, and the average standard error of estimate for the affective component is 3.80, or a fairly stable measure. However, the average error of estimate for the policy component is 18.83 or a relatively unstable opinion distribution.[4] The affective element varies little over time supporting Proposition 5a, attitudes remain unchanged between polls. However, attitudes toward unity are volatile which supports Proposition 5b with moodiness reflected in considerable change between opinion samplings.

Linkage Between Attitudes and Transactions. In addition to ascertaining the nature of certain mass attitudes, we must examine the linkage between attitudes and transactions. Deutsch (1962, 212–215) asserts that transactional exchange will lead to more receptive attitudes toward other nations and integration efforts. This should be especially noticeable for transactions which stress interpersonal contact such as tourism and student exchange (I. Galtung).

The impact of transactional exchange upon the affective and policy components of attitudes can be examined over a limited number of years and a longer time-interval to determine if length of time is an important element. To determine if Proposition 6a, asserting the congruence of the two strains, is correct, the correlations between transactional exchanges in 1952 and the affective and policy components of opinion in 1955 and 1964 are examined in Table 6.2.

TABLE 6.2

The Impact of Transactions in 1952 Upon Attitudes in 1955 and 1964

	MAIL	STUD	TELG	TOUR	TRAD
Affective Component	.27 (.26)	.29 (.18)	.11 (.02)	.10 (.04)	.27 (.22)
Policy Component	.02 (.07)	.02 (.06)	.01 (.02)	.01 (.01)	.01 (.01)

The correlations for 1952 transactions and 1955 attitudes are presented first, those for 1952 transactions and 1964 attitudes are in parentheses.

3. The formula for the standard error of estimate is

$$S_{y.x} = S_y \sqrt{1 - r^2}$$

where S_y is the standard deviation.

4. This would mean that given any point on an opinion distribution one could predict the other points within plus or minus three percentage points for the affective component and plus or minus eighteen percentage points for the policy component. This means a range of six and thirty-six percentage points respectively. The former is narrow, the latter much too expansive to make accurate predictions.

The evidence tends to support Proposition 6b that transactional exchange does not predict to the affective component of opinion. In terms of a three-year interval, none of the transactions is correlated with the affective component at a level of .3. None is significant at the .05 level, but the multiple correlation coefficient for all five variables predicting to the affective component is .47 in 1955 and .50 in 1964.[5]

However, interpersonal exchange is not that highly interrelated with ensuing opinions. Tourism has only a negligible impact and only student exchange at a three-year interval has a correlation of near .3. The long-term impact of interpersonal exchange at an aggregative level is not apparent. The salience of mail as a predictor of opinion patterns reinforces Deutsch's notion (1960a, 147–150) that information exchange is an important predictor of mass attitudes; he argues that increased mail exchange between countries which occurred in this time interval increased the visibility of the other country in a dyadic relationship.

In terms of other aspects of attitudinal integration, there is no evidence to suggest any impact of transactional exchange on ensuing perceptions of regional unity. In neither the three-year nor the twelve-year periods is there any correlation above .1; most hover near .01. The multiple correlation coefficient is not much higher, with .03 for three years and .09 for the twelve-year interval. Transactional exchange predicts to ensuing positive affect rather than policy outlooks.

However, are the primacies of mail as the key predictor and of transactions as general indicators of future attitudinal distributions generalizable to other time-periods? To investigate the primacy of exchange of communications rather than people, another time-interval to be examined would be the period from 1958–1960, when supranational institutions were created and their impact on ensuing transactional exchange. The impact of transactions in 1958 upon attitudes in 1964 reveals the following pattern. Only trade and mail have correlations above .2 with .27 and .25 respectively.[6] The multiple correlation for all transactions upon the affective component in 1964 is .41.[7] Again the primacy of the exchange of people is not shown, as neither student exchange nor tourism is that closely linked with the affective component of opinion with no correlation above .2. This may suggest that exchange of communications may be more important over a decade in creating a favorable opinion environ-

5. Multiple correlations are useful when one has more than one predictor (in this case, five) and one criterion. For a discussion of the formula for computing the multiple correlation, see Cooley and Lohnes (1962). The multiple correlation cannot be smaller than any of the component bivariate correlations.
6. None of the correlation coefficients on a bivariate basis was significant at the .05 level.
7. The multiple correlation coefficient for the 1958–1961 period was .43, with mail having the highest coefficient of .26.

ment than other forms of interaction. Perhaps student exchange and tourism involve proportionately such a small subcomponent of the population that their impact will be seen only over several decades.[8]

In terms of the impact on the policy component, the result is again negligible with no correlation above .10 and a multiple correlation of .04 for the 1958–1961 interval and .07 for the 1958–1964 period. The length of the time interval does not appear to be a key consideration in determining the maximum impact of transactions upon either the affective or the policy components.

In addition to the impact of transactional exchange upon opinion patterns, to what extent is the relationship reciprocal? The impact of attitudinal integration on transactions is minimal as seen for two different time-intervals, 1955 and 1964, with the correlations presented in Table 6.3.

None of the correlations between the components of attitudinal integration related very strongly to ensuing transactions in 1955 or 1964. The highest correlation between the affective component and trade in 1955 is only .13. The relationship between the two measures seems to be that transactions tend to predict to attitudes, with the most important forms of cooperation appearing to be exchange of goods (trade) and information (mail).

A second aspect of the relationship between transactions and atti-

TABLE 6.3

The Impact of Mass Opinion in 1952 upon Transactions in 1955 and 1964

	AFFECTIVE COMPONENT	POLICY COMPONENT
Mail	.07 (.06)	.02 (.01)
Stud	.14 (.10)	.01 (.01)
Telg	.04 (.02)	.06 (.03)
Tour	.10 (.10)	.01 (.02)
Trad	.13 (.11)	.05 (.02)

The first figures represent 1955, those in parentheses 1964. The two time-periods were selected to give a maximum range of impact in the short run (three years) and long run (twelve years). None of the correlations presented is significant at the .05 level.

8. Such a study is not possible given the available data, but in another decade, a more accurate appraisal can be made of the long-term impact of tourism and student exchange.

tudes at an aggregative level is the impact of cooperation on the extent to which dyadic perceptions are equivalent. Scott and Etzioni both argue that one of the consequences of increasing interaction is a reduction in the gap between reciprocal perceptions. Attributions of positive affect toward other nations in Western Europe became more prevalent with the passage of time in the 1950's (Etzioni, 1965, 265–267).

In examining the validity of this notion, the conclusion must be tempered because there are only eleven dyads[9] in the study on which there is data on reciprocal perceptions over the period 1952–1964. In analyzing these dyads, the reciprocal positive perceptions were subtracted from one another to find the differences, and then the average discrepancy was found for each of the three-year periods.[10] This information is presented in Table 6.4.

There is some support for Proposition 7a, a high rate of transactional exchange does lead to closer reciprocal perceptions. Although the gap between pairs increases between 1952 and 1955, a steady decline follows reaching a discrepancy of 10 percent in 1964. However, it should be noted that in most of these pairs, at least half the populace perceives the other nation with positive affect. The only exception is the France–Great Britain dyad, where British attributions of positive affect toward the French dropped, with the descent beginning in the 1950's when de Gaulle gained power (Hoffman).[11]

TABLE 6.4

The Amount of Average Percentage Discrepancy in Reciprocal Perceptions for Three-Year Intervals

	1952	1955	1958	1961	1964
Discrepancy	13%	.16%	.14%	11%	10%

9. The eleven dyads are United States–France, United States–West Germany, United States–Great Britain, United States–Italy, Denmark–Norway, France–West Germany, France–Italy, France–Great Britain, West Germany–Italy, West Germany–Great Britain, and Italy–Great Britain.
10. These are percentage figures. For example, if 62 percent of the British perceived the United States with positive affect and 50 percent of the Americans so viewed the British, there would be a discrepancy of 12 percent. This figure was computed for each pair and then averaged for each of the five years examined.
11. British positive affect toward the French dropped to its lowest point in 1964, with 15 percent perceiving the French favorably and a slightly higher level for French attribution of positive affect toward the British.

Cultural Like shared political values, cultural homo-
Homogeneity and geneity is often cited as a factor making for
Mutual Relevance the sort of mutuality of understanding and
feelings which breeds mutual involvement.
Thus, we have offered the hypothesis that the greater the cultural homo-
geneity of two countries, the greater their mutual behavioral relevance
(Proposition 8a). We found that theorists of no less stature than Morgen-
thau have disputed this contention. Their argument suggests that cultural
factors are largely irrelevant to the patterns of international behavior.
Accordingly, this position is taken as a counterhypothesis.

The results of an empirical analysis of the relationship between
homogeneity and patterns of mutual relevance are shown in Table 6.5.
Again the results lend support for the positively directed hypothesis, but
the indicated relationship is somewhat less than might have been
expected.

TABLE 6.5

Cultural Homogeneity as a Predictor of Mutual Relevance

BIVARIATE CORRELATIONS			
Inter-Predictor:	*Rac Hom*	*Rel Hom*	*Lang Hom*
Racial Homogeneity	1.00	.12	.12
Religious Homogeneity	.12	1.00	.30
Language Homogeneity	.12	.30	1.00

Predictor-Criterion:								
	Mail	*Telg*	*Telp*	*Telx*	*Trad*	*Stud*	*Tour*	*NGO*
Rac Hom	.15	.14	.13	.13	.14	.14	.15	.28
Rel Hom	.19	.18	.19	.12	.11	.10	.17	.25
Lang Hom	.28	.23	.26	.08	.16	.16	.27	.17

CANONICAL SOLUTIONS

First Solution: $Rc_{max} = .43$

Predictor Weightings[a]			Criterion Weightings[a]			
Rac Hom	Rel Hom	Lang Hom	Mail	Telg	Telp	Telx
.51	.46	.51	.35	.13	.14	−.08
			Trad	Stud	Tour	NGO
			−.32	.06	.29	.68

Second Solution: $Rc_2 = .19$

Predictor Weightings[a]			Criterion Weightings[a]			
Rac Hom	Rel Hom	Lang Hom	Mail	Telg	Telp	Telx
.59	.40	−.89	−.43	−.08	−.17	.23
			Trad	Stud	Tour	NGO
			.12	−.05	−.41	.78

Third Solution: $Rc_3 = .08$

[a] Coefficients are for standardized measures.

The optimal canonical solution suggests that cultural homogeneity, like shared political values, tends to have its greatest impact on mutual relevance through common NGO memberships, although its influence is considerably more widely distributed than was the case for political-value homogeneity. Although of negligible importance as a behavioral tendency, the relational pattern indicated in the second canonical solution shows rather clearly that language heterogeneity can have a detrimental effect on inter-nation communications, most notably on mail and tourist travel.

The general conclusion which we draw from the results presented in Table 6.5 is that cultural homogeneity tends to foster greater mutual relevance, but that its influence is, at best, a moderate one. This support for Proposition 8a is somewhat reassuring in the sense that substantial cooperative involvement in the international milieu can exist in the face of considerable heterogeneity.

Common Historical Experience Common historical experience is allegedly another possible source of common identifications and mutual predictability which may promote mutual relevance. Our first hypothesis (Proposition 9a) suggests that commonality of age, of colonial experience—either as colonizers or colonized—and of internal stability will tend to promote intercourse between nations. The null counterpart (Proposition 9b) is based on the contention that the tangled web of history has left no such neat pattern of affinities, rather it has produced both enmity and amity with the net effect being that common historical experience has little or no bearing on mutual relevance.

On the basis of the results presented in Table 6.6, we are almost prone to accept the latter position, the .29 first canonical solution notwithstanding. Certainly the most striking aspect of the findings reported in the table is the tenuousness of the relationship between historical experience and mutual relevance.

In interpreting what meager relation there is, both the first and second canonical solutions indicate interesting patterns. The influence of shared historical attributes on mutual relevance is manifested primarily through common NGO memberships, the dominant predictor pattern being seen in nations of comparable age and historical stability, but of heterogeneous colonial experience. The second canonical solution indicates a behavioral tendency almost as strong as the first and provides an interesting commentary on the impact that common historical attributes have on student exchange in particular. The prevailing pattern is clearly for historically more heterogeneous countries to have the greatest student exchange. This is consistent with the common observation that the elites

TABLE 6.6

Common Historical Experience as a Predictor of Mutual Relevance

BIVARIATE CORRELATIONS

Inter-Predictor:	Rel Age	Colon	Gen Stab
Relative Age	1.00	−.03	−.03
Colonialism	−.03	1.00	−.09
General Stability	−.03	−.09	1.00

Predictor-Criterion:

	Mail	Telg	Telp	Telx	Trad	Stud	Tour	NGO
Rel Age	.05	.08	.08	.08	.05	.05	.10	.14
Colon	.00	.02	.00	−.04	−.11	−.17	.02	−.15
Gen Stab	.08	.05	.08	.08	.08	−.01	.10	.17

CANONICAL SOLUTIONS

First Solution: $Rc_{max} = .29$

Predictor Weightings[a]			Criterion Weightings[a]			
Rel Age	Colon	Gen Stab	Mail	Telg	Telp	Telx
.48	−.66	.64	−.05	−.25	.08	−.03
			Trad	Stud	Tour	NGO
			.09	.13	.07	.96

Second Solution: $Rc_2 = .23$

Predictor Weightings[a]			Criterion Weightings[a]			
Rel Age	Colon	Gen Stab	Mail	Telg	Telp	Telx
.34	.75	.53	.22	.23	.20	.30
			Trad	Stud	Tour	NGO
			−.21	−1.03	.49	.08

Third Solution: $Rc_3 = .09$

[a] Coefficients are for standardized measures.

in many relatively new and formerly colonial nations which are struggling for stability were trained in mother, or colonizing, nations. This observation is, of course, attenuated by the weakness of the overall relationship.

All in all, a degree of influence may appropriately be attributed to common historical experience in terms of mutual relevance (i.e., support for Proposition 9a). But this influence is at best exceedingly limited and perhaps of negligible importance.

Another facet of historical experience worthy of examination is the extent to which a vestige of conflict remains salient in a system. In assessing the impact of the Second World War, Buchanan and Cantril (38–44) assert that the impact of war lingered far beyond the cessation of hostilities in 1945, particularly in the North Atlantic region. The extent to which there is positive affect generated between countries can be traced to whether nations were allies or adversaries during the war (Buchanan and Cantril; Hoffman).

In determining the relationship between alliance patterns and the amount of positive affect generated between opinion dyads, a product-moment correlation was computed for the 1952 affective component of .19.[12] Buchanan and Cantril (38–44) argue that the relationship should decline with the passage of time as the war experience becomes less vivid in the public memory. The correlation is .10 in 1955, .04 in 1958, .03 in 1961, and .04 in 1964. The latter contention of declining salience is supported; however, the impact of alignment patterns on opinions is not as strong as alleged, reaching only .19. A similar pattern is found in examining the war impact on the policy component, with no correlation for the five years examined above .12.[13] As a consequence, the evidence supports Proposition 9b that wartime alignments have little impact on opinion distributions in the ensuing years.

In examining the impact of the war on transaction patterns, Russett (1965, 162–195) asserts that the impact of the conflict should be present, but mitigated with the passage of time. The correlations between war alignments and transactions in 1952 and 1964 are presented in Table 6.7.

The results confirm Proposition 9a for the war impact on ensuing transaction patterns, particularly in tourism (.54) and exchange of mail (.50) in 1952 as well as a decade later. However, there is no evidence

TABLE 6.7

The Relationship Between the Impact of the Second World War and Transactions in 1952 and 1964

	1952 TRANSACTIONS	1964 TRANSACTIONS
Mail	.50	.51
Stud	.29	.34
Telg	.38	.37
Telx	. . .	.35
Tour	.54	.56
Trad	.36	.45

12. None of the correlations presented is significant at the .05 level for the affective component. A positive correlation in the predicted direction is due to the way that alignment patterns were coded. The more likely that two nations were allies, the greater the likelihood that positive affect between the publics will occur.
13. None of the correlations concerning the policy component was significant at the

that the impact of the war has lessened since the correlations remain high. It appears that wartime allies such as the United States, Great Britain, and France tend to cooperate more with each other than with wartime enemies such as West Germany. As a consequence, the principal background factors contributing to predicting transactional exchange are previous integrative experience and the impact of war. In contrast, proximity, which had some impact on the affective components of attitudes, is not that salient in predicting transactional exchange.

Commonality and
Level of Social
Welfare and
Mutual Relevance

We suspect that most people would agree that health is preferable to sickness, that education is better than ignorance, and that employment is better than unemployment. Nonetheless, there are marked differences among nations in the extent to which these social welfare values have been realized. We have presented hypotheses which argue that the greater the homogeneity of two nations in terms of realized social welfare and the greater the average level of welfare realization, the greater these nations' mutual relevance. The rationale behind the first hypothesis (Proposition 10a) is in keeping with the general notion that commonality of perspectives and immediate interests will tend to foster mutual behavioral relevance. The second hypothesis (Proposition 10b) is predicated on the assumption that welfare realization enhances the instrumental capacity of a nation to interact with other states and the greater the level of social welfare within two nations, the more likely they are to engage one another internationally.

In juxtaposition to these contentions, we offered arguments to suggest that (Proposition 10c) the near-universality of social welfare values may breed intercourse between the most- and least-developed nations in terms of welfare realization and that the common aspiration to insure a decent life for all men may blur any hierarchical pattern of transnational behavior.

Table 6.8 shows the results of an empirical analysis of the first hypothesis for the year 1955. Although the individual bivariate correlations are not impressive, the overall pattern is clear: the more homogeneous two nations in terms of realized social welfare, the greater their mutual relevance in least in terms of common NGO memberships (support for Proposition 10a).

The effect of the level of welfare development of two nations on patterns of mutual relevance is shown in Table 6.9. The results are generally consistent with those regarding welfare homogeneity and lend support to our second hypothesis (Proposition 10b). Mutual relevance, primarily manifested through common NGO memberships, tends to be greater among nations with the least unemployment and greatest educational opportunity.

There is, of course, overlapping in our two findings regarding the effects of realized social welfare. Both homogeneity and average level of welfare realization are, however, important. As indicated in the canonical solution presented in Table 6.10, both sets of factors contribute almost equally to the mutual relevance of two nations. Collectively, they produce a maximum canonical correlation of .59.

Homogeneity and Average Level of Socioeconomic Development Theorists are generally much more optimistic in their assessments of the prospects for involvement among socioeconomically developed countries than among less-developed ones. Their reasoning is very similar to that regarding the level of welfare realization. Presumably, development

TABLE 6.8

Social Welfare Homogeneity as a Predictor of Mutual Relevance

BIVARIATE CORRELATIONS			
Inter-Predictor:	% Unempl	% Prim Ed	Pers/Phys
% Unemployed	1.00	−.03	.03
% Primary Education	−.03	1.00	.53
Persons/Physician	.03	.53	1.00

Predictor-Criterion:	Mail	Telg	Telp	Telx	Trad	Stud	Tour	NGO
% Unempl	.07	.04	.03	.00	.07	.04	.03	.16
% Prim Ed	.16	.15	.16	.23	.16	.08	.14	.37
Per/Phys	.14	.16	.15	.22	.18	.13	.12	.46

CANONICAL SOLUTIONS

First Solution: $Rc_{max} = .52$

Predictor Weightings[a]			Criterion Weightings[a]			
% Unempl	%Prim Ed	Per/Phys	Mail	Telg	Telp	Telx
.29	.41	.66	.13	−.02	.10	.10
			Trad	Stud	Tour	NGO
			−.07	−.16	−.06	.98

Second Solution: $Rc_2 = .12$
Third Solution: $Rc_3 = .08$

[a] Coefficients are for standardized measures.

TABLE 6.9

Level of Social Welfare as a Predictor of Mutual Relevance

BIVARIATE CORRELATIONS

Inter-Predictor:	% Unempl	% Prim Ed	Per/Phys
% Unemployed	1.00	−.06	−.09
% Primary Ed	−.06	1.00	−.31
Persons/Phys	−.09	−.31	1.00

Predictor-Criterion:

	Mail	Telg	Telp	Telx	Trad	Stud	Tour	NGO
% Unempl	−.03	−.05	−.02	−.07	−.09	−.02	.03	−.11
% Prim Ed	.07	.12	.08	.24	.23	.20	.06	.43
Per/Phys	−.05	−.05	−.04	−.09	−.07	−.04	−.03	−.26

CANONICAL SOLUTIONS

First Solution: $Rc_{max} = .51$

Predictor Weightings[a]			Criterion Weightings[a]			
% Unempl	% Prim Ed	Per/Phys	Mail	Telg	Telp	Telx
−.15	.50	−.04	−.10	−.02	−.11	.04
			Trad	Stud	Tour	NGO
			.32	.28	−.25	.79

Second Solution: $Rc_2 = .13$
Third Solution: $Rc_3 = .10$

[a] Coefficients are for standardized measures.

TABLE 6.10

Homogeneity and Average Level of Welfare Considered Simultaneously as Predictors of Mutual Relevance

First Canonical Solution: $Rc_{max} = .59$

	Predictor Weightings[a]			Criterion Weightings[a]			
Homo:	% Unempl	% Prim Ed	Per/Phys	Mail	Telg	Telp	Telx
	.29	.17	.19	.00	.00	−.01	.09
Mean:	% Unempl	% Prim Ed	Per/Phys	Trad	Stud	Tour	NGO
	−.21	.50	−.03	.09	−.05	−.13	.97

[a] Coefficients are for standardized measures.

enhances both the capacity and inclination for transnational relations. Thus, our first hypothesis (Proposition 11a) is the greater the average level of internal socioeconomic development within a dyad, the greater the dyad's mutual relevance.

The second hypothesis (Proposition 11b) is somewhat related to the first. It is based on the assumption that the level of development within a nation may be the source of common identifications and functional interests with nations at a like state of development (i.e., shared problems will tend to foster common interests). Thus, the assumption that homogeneous development leads to mutual relevance.

The third hypothesis (Proposition 11c) offered with respect to socioeconomic development is the null form of the first two. Its underlying arguments are twofold. First, dependency relations, including colonial ties, still exist between many developed and underdeveloped countries. These may be transformed into very strong and abiding bonds, as in the case of the British Commonwealth. Secondly, whether from moral compunction or strategic Cold War considerations, many developed nations have felt obliged to aid and uplift less-developed ones. The net effect of all this, our hypothesis suggests, is that homogeneity and average level of development will exhibit no effect on manifest patterns of mutual relevance.

An empirical assessment of the first hypothesis (Proposition 11a) is presented in Table 6.11. The results contained within the table show a substantial relation to exist between the level of internal development and mutual relevance. The relational patterns represented in the canonical solutions are, however, difficult to decipher. The dominant pattern as indicated by the variable weightings associated with the first canonical solution seems to suggest that the most mutually active nations are those which are becoming increasingly industrialized (i.e., less agriculturally based) and increasingly literate, but which have not yet attained high per capita wealth. As nations become wealthier, they apparently tend either to spread their attention or to become more isolationist, although some forms of relative interaction may increase, most notably tourism.

Although the second canonical solution marks a much less pronounced behavioral tendency and presents us with a rather confusing pattern of predictor weightings, it seems to indicate the pattern of mutual relevance between less-developed and more developed nations. As we interpret the weightings, they are the peculiar result of averaging extremes: developed characteristics being this regression interpretation, the overall pattern that emerges seems quite reasonable. The mutual relevance between developed and underdeveloped nations tends to be manifested in the forms of student exchange, trade, and mail. These

TABLE 6.11

Average Level of Socio-Economic Development as a Predictor of Mutual Relevance

BIVARIATE CORRELATIONS

Inter-Predictor:

	% Agric	Illit	Urban	Income
% Agriculture	1.00	.78	−.70	−.76
Illiteracy	.78	1.00	−.61	−.59
Urbanization	−.70	−.61	1.00	.54
Net Income/cap	−.76	−.59	.54	1.00

Predictor-Criterion:

	Mail	Telg	Telp	Telx	Trad	Stud	Tour	NGO
% Agric	−.13	−.16	−.10	−.28	−.32	−.22	−.04	−.54
Illit	−.08	−.15	−.09	−.29	−.28	−.21	−.09	−.53
Urban	.15	.15	.14	.21	.32	.32	.06	.39
Income	.12	.13	.07	.20	.28	.19	.05	.35

CANONICAL SOLUTIONS

First Solution: $Rc_{max} = .60$

Predictor Weightings[a]

% Agric	Illit	Urban	Income
−.73	−.41	.06	−.18

Criterion Weightings[a]

Mail	Telg	Telp	Telx
−.09	.00	−.12	.11
Trad	**Stud**	**Tour**	**NGO**
.29	.04	−.22	.88

Second Solution: $Rc_2 = .27$

Predictor Weightings[a]

% Agric	Illit	Urban	Income
−.68	−.61	−1.30	−.42

Criterion Weightings[a]

Mail	Telg	Telp	Telx
−.24	.16	.04	.34
Trad	**Stud**	**Tour**	**NGO**
−.34	−.92	.28	.35

Third Solution: $Rc_3 = .15$

Fourth Solution: $Rc_4 = .14$

[a] Coefficients are for standardized measures.

dyads tend not to have intercourse along the other dimensions of transnational behavior.

This interpretation is, indeed, borne out when we look at the effects of developmental homogeneity on patterns of mutual relevance. As can be seen from the first canonical solution in Table 6.12, developmental heterogeneity tends to foster student exchange, although other indicators of mutual relevance tend to be associated with developmental homogeneity. It is interesting to note the effect of agricultural heterogeneity, particularly as it is shown in the second solution. While it obviously tends to reduce telephone communications, agricultural heterogeneity tends to promote trade, thus indicating the continuing importance of economic specialization. Specialization is opposed to exploitation because the predictor pattern suggests that the dyads involved tend to be relatively homogeneous with respect to literacy and urbanization.

Excepting agriculture, the overall effect of developmental homogeneity on mutual relevance is consonant with our second hypothesis (Proposition 11b), even though the relationship is not a particularly strong one. The tendency is for developmentally homogeneous nations to show the greatest mutual relevance. As might be expected, there is considerable overlap between our findings with respect to developmental

TABLE 6.12

Developmental Homogeneity as a Predictor of Mutual Relevance

BIVARIATE CORRELATIONS

Inter-Predictor:	% Agric	Illit	Urban	Income
% Agric	1.00	.47	.35	.46
Illit	.47	1.00	.17	.35
Urban	.35	.17	1.00	.35
Income	.46	.35	.35	1.00

Predictor-Criterion:

	Mail	Telg	Telp	Telx	Trad	Stud	Tour	NGO
% Agric	.06	.03	.12	.03	−.06	−.06	.13	.02
Illit	.18	.12	.19	.20	.11	.06	.15	.11
Urban	.08	.07	.11	.10	.06	.06	.10	.17
Income	.13	.10	.17	.15	.09	−.02	.18	.17

CANONICAL SOLUTIONS

First Solution: $Rc_{max} = .34$

Predictor Weightings[a]

% Agric	Illit	Urban	Income
−.24	.62	.23	.63

Criterian Weightings[a]

Mail	Telg	Telp	Telx
.38	−.15	.32	.55

Trad	Stud	Tour	NGO
−.07	−.51	.21	.38

Second Solution: $Rc_2 = .22$

Predictor Weightings[a]

% Agric	Illit	Urban	Income
−1.18	.44	.34	.00

Criterian Weightings[a]

Mail	Telg	Telp	Telx
.17	.03	−.71	.18

Trad	Stud	Tour	NGO
.80	.15	−.46	.12

Third Solution: $Rc_3 = .14$
Fourth Solution: $Rc_4 = .11$

[a] Coefficients are for standardized measures.

homogeneity and those for average level of development. The latter (Proposition 11a) is clearly a much more important predictor of mutual relevance; but as Table 6.13 indicates both factors (Propositions 12a, 12b) are important.

Stability of Political Three different hypotheses have been ad-
Regimes and vanced regarding the effects of regime stabil-
Mutual Relevance ity on patterns of inter-nation intercourse. The
first (Proposition 12a) asserts that both mutual predictability and attention capabilities are enhanced the longer a given set of decision-makers are in office, and thus that those dyads with the greater average regime stability will tend to show the most mutual relevance. The second hypothesis (Proposition 12b) notes, however, that faultering regimes may seek to stabilize themselves by promoting relations with countries having more stable regimes. Therefore, nations heterogeneous in terms of stability would tend to interact. The third position (Proposition 12c) is predicated on a functional argument which suggests that owing to a commonality of problems, less stable regimes may attempt to find solutions to mutual problems by promoting cooperative ties and identifications with one another, while the more stable nations tend to interact among themselves. Thus, homogeneity in terms of political stability leads to mutual relevance.

Although the various arguments seem sufficiently convincing, the results yielded by our analysis fail to offer support for any of them. With respect to the hypothesis linking average level of regime stability and mutual relevance (Proposition 12a), we obtain a multiple correlation of only .06. The homogeneity-heterogeneity hypotheses (Propositions 12b, 12c) fare even worse. The multiple R between homogeneity in terms of political stability and mutual relevance is a miniscule .02.

While it is possible that some effect is washed out in the aggregate

TABLE 6.13

*Homogeneity and Average Level of Development Considered
Simultaneously as Predictors of Mutual Relevance*

First Canonical Solution: $Rc_{max} = .65$

	Predictor Weightings[a]				Criterion Weightings[a]			
	% Agric	Illit	Urban	Income	Mail	Telg	Telp	Telx
Homo:	.03	.36	−.02	.10	.01	−.04	−.03	.23
Mean:	−.67	−.43	.09	−.17	Trad	Stud	Tour	NGO
					.23	−.05	−.16	.84

[a] Coefficients are for standardized measures.

because of conflicting tendencies, we think it highly unlikely that any substantial effect would not be shown through either the dyadic average regime stability or homogeneity measure. We are, therefore, forced to conclude that regime stability is largely irrelevant to international patterns of mutual relevance. The patterns of interaction between states seem impervious to the longevity of a given set of political office-holders.

Military Power and   The military power of a state is another so-
Mutual Relevance   cietal factor which presumably affects its international intercourse. In reviewing the litera-
ture on the effects of military power, we found two strands of thought. The first (Proposition 13a) contends that similarity of military powers leads to mutual relevance. The rationale is tied to interaction capabilities. Supposedly, the greater the military power of a state, the greater its capability to interact with other states without jeopardizing its autonomy (i.e., it can and will seek to avoid repugnant dependency ties). The second hypothesis (Proposition 13b) suggests that weaker states will augment their security through relations with stronger ones and/or stronger states will attempt to prevent weaker states from falling into hostile spheres of influence. Thus, heterogeneity in military capability will lead to mutual relevance.

Our analysis reveals limited support for the first hypothesis (Proposition 13a). As can be seen from Table 6.14, militarily stronger dyads tend to show the greatest mutual relevance. This result represents primarily the effect of the level of military power within a dyad rather than that of the degree of military homogeneity. The maximum canonical correlation between mutual relevance and military homogeneity, per se, is only .36, which is considered sufficient to reject the second hypothesis (Proposition 13b), but otherwise negligible.

The behavioral pattern indicated by the first solution in Table 6.14 is fairly clear. Militarily stronger dyads tend to exhibit greater mutual mobility and trade but less communications than militarily weaker dyads. Although almost negligible as a behavioral tendency, the pattern indicated in the second canonical solution seems to suggest that nations with the best equipped armies (i.e., larger defense expenditures, but fewer military personnel) tend to have contact, particularly through NGOs, but do not tend to trade with one another. This may be taken as something of a Cold War effect.

The basic conclusion flowing from our analysis, however, is simply that military power has rather limited influence on patterns of transnational intercourse. What influence it does have is manifested in a tendency in which the greater the average level of military power between two nations, the greater their mutual relevance.

TABLE 6.14

Average Level of Military Power as a Predictor of Mutual Relevance

BIVARIATE CORRELATIONS

Inter-Predictor:

	Number in Military
Defense Expenditure	.14

Predictor-Criterion:

	Mail	Telg	Telp	Telx	Trad	Stud	Tour	NGO
Def Ex	.05	.06	.06	.09	.13	.24	.12	.22
No in Mil	.07	.08	.05	.09	.21	.22	.09	.07

CANONICAL SOLUTIONS

First Solution: $Rc_{max} = .36$

Predictor Weightings[a]		Criterion Weightings[a]			
Def Ex	No in Mil	Mail	Telg	Telp	Telx
.77	.54	−.17	−.10	−.44	−.13
		Trad	Stud	Tour	NGO
		.24	.85	.31	.36

Second Solution: $Rc_2 = .19$

Predictor Weightings[a]		Criterion Weightings[a]			
Def Ex	No in Mil	Mail	Telg	Telp	Telx
.66	−.85	−.02	−.19	.50	−.18
		Trad	Stud	Tour	NGO
		−1.13	.15	.04	.92

[a] Coefficients are for standardized measures.

Economic Power and Mutual Relevance   Many theorists agree that the economic capabilities, real and potential, of a nation will have important bearing on its patterns of international involvement. We found, however, that there is much less agreement on the way in which this influence will be manifested. From the standpoint of action capabilities, it would seem the greater the average economic capacity of a nation-pair, the greater their probable interaction (Proposition 14a). But from a supply-and-demand perspective, one might reasonably argue that the more heterogeneous two nations in economic capacity, the more they are likely to exhibit mutual relevance (Proposition 14c). From yet another point of view (viz., common functional interests), it seems reasonable to believe that the more homogeneous two nations in terms of economic capabilities, the greater their mutual behavioral relevance (Proposition 14b).

Our analysis offers moderate support for the first hypothesis (Proposition 14a). Dyads with greater average economic power tend to show greater mutual relevance. The pattern indicated in the first canonical solution in Table 6.15 seems to suggest that the most mutually active nations are those with the greatest realized economic capacities (i.e., greater GNPs and less energy potential). Such nations tend to trade more, exchange more students, and have more common NGO memberships.

The above relationship must be considered largely the result of the level of economic power, rather than the degree of homogeneity between the nations. As can be seen from Table 6.16, economic homogeneity has a relatively slight and highly mixed influence of patterns of inter-nation intercourse. In fact, the behavioral pattern indicated in the first solution shown in Table 6.16 suggests that with the exceptions of telephone communications and common NGO memberships, heterogeneity at least with respect to GNP tends to foster interaction. The overall effect of economic homogeneity and heterogeneity, however, is so small that we would give little weight to either the second or third hypotheses (Propositions 14b, 14c).

The general conclusion we would draw regarding economic power is that nations with the greatest realized economic capabilities tend to show the most mutual relevance.

TABLE 6.15

Average Level of Economic Power as a Predictor of Mutual Relevance

BIVARIATE CORRELATIONS							
Inter-Predictor:		Eng Pot			GNP		
Energy Potential		1.00			.92		
GNP		.92			1.00		
Predictor-Criterion:							
	Mail	Telg	Telp	Telx	Trad	Stud	Tour	NGO
Eng Pot	.09	.09	.07	.08	.23	.25	.09	.07
GNP	.09	.10	.04	.00	.13	.12	.05	.08

CANONICAL SOLUTIONS

First Solution: $Rc_{max} = .43$

Predictor Weightings[a]		Criterion Weightings[a]			
Eng Pot	GNP	Mail	Telg	Telp	Telx
−1.42	2.14	.03	−.04	−.21	−.19
		Trad	Stud	Tour	NGO
		.26	.88	−.21	.35

Second Solution: $Rc_2 = .16$

[a] Coefficients are for standardized measures.

TABLE 6.16

Homogeneity of Economic Power as a Predictor of Mutual Relevance

BIVARIATE CORRELATIONS

Inter-Predictor:

	Relative Energy Potential
Relative GNP	.30

Predictor-Criterion:

	Mail	Telg	Telp	Telx	Trad	Stud	Tour	NGO
Rel Eng Pot	−.01	−.03	−.02	−.01	−.04	−.05	.02	.00
Rel GNP	−.02	−.01	.01	.01	−.03	−.10	.00	.16

CANONICAL SOLUTIONS

First Solution: $Rc_{max} = .24$

Predictor Weightings[a]		Criterion Weightings[a]			
Rel Eng Pot	Rel GNP	Mail	Telg	Telp	Telx
−.19	1.04	−.14	−.02	−.53	−.09
		Trad	Stud	Tour	NGO
		−.26	−.61	−.21	1.01

Second Solution: $Rc_2 = .08$

[a] Coefficients are for standardized measures.

Bureaucratic Bureaucratic capabilities, like the other so-
Capabilities and cietal factors, are presumably an indicator of
Mutual Relevance the capacity of two nations to act and inter-
act. In fact, a number of scholars including
Deutsch assert that well-developed bureaucratic, or administrative, capa-
bilities are crucial to mutually responsive relations between nations.

Accordingly, we offered a twofold hypothesis (Proposition 15a) that
the greater and more homogeneous the bureaucratic capabilities of two
nations, the greater their relative intercourse. The results presented in
Table 6.17 do, indeed, support Proposition 15a.

Two observations can be made concerning the first solution shown
in the table. First, in terms of influencing mutual relevance, the average
level of bureaucratic development is clearly more important than inter-
nation homogeneity. In the best canonical solution, the coefficient for the
average level of bureaucratic development is roughly three times as large
as that for the homogeneity measure. When considered individually,
these two factors produced with the eight indicators of mutual relevance
multiple correlations of .55 and .41, respectively. Secondly, the dominant
effect of homogeneous and highly developed bureaucratic capabilities
tends to be manifested through trade and common NGO memberships.

Although accounting for relatively little behavior, the second canonical solution presents a rather interesting pattern. It indicates that the relations between more heterogeneous nations in terms of bureaucratic capabilities tend to take the form of trade and student exchange, while relations among more homogeneous, but somewhat less-developed, nations tend to be in the form of interpersonal communications and tourism. In general, Table 6.17 indicates that homogeneous bureaucratic capabilities of two nations leads to greater mutual relevance.

Conclusion   A number of societal properties have been examined to determine their predictive power with respect to ensuing mutual relevance. In general, the pattern for both the regional and global studies was that these properties did not have the impact which many theorists claim. At best, there was a weak, not a strong, link between unit properties and variables indicating mutual relevance.

TABLE 6.17

Homogeneity and Average Level of Bureaucratic Development as Predictors of Mutual Relevance

BIVARIATE CORRELATIONS

Inter-Predictor:

	Homogeneity of Bureaucracy
Level of Bureaucracy	.05

Predictor-Criterion:

	Mail	Telg	Telp	Telx	Trad	Stud	Tour	NGO
Bureau Lev	.11	.12	.10	.25	.27	.21	.07	.53
Bureau Hom	.17	.16	.18	.15	.14	.05	.20	.23

CANONICAL SOLUTIONS

First Solution: $Rc_{max} = .58$

Predictor Weightings[a]		Criterion Weightings[a]			
Bureau Lev	Bureau Hom	Mail	Telg	Telp	Telx
.93	.32	.01	−.09	−.08	.08
		Trad	Stud	Tour	NGO
		.20	−.01	−.06	.93

Second Solution: $Rc_2 = .22$

Predictor Weightings[a]		Criterion Weightings[a]			
Bureau Lev	Bureau Hom	Mail	Telg	Telp	Telx
.37	−.95	−.35	−.22	−.29	−.18
		Trad	Stud	Tour	NGO
		.31	.63	−.61	.07

[a] Coefficients are for standardized measures.

chapter 7

Systems Properties and Mutual Relevance

Introduction   The final set of background factors which we
seek to relate to patterns of mutual relevance
concerns systems properties. In particular, we are interested in systemic
indicators of past memories and habits of mutual attention. The general
model outlined in the first chapter assumes that these patterns will be
evidenced in the intensity and extensity of previous collaborative experience.

Previous   A number of leading scholars have persua-
Collaborative   sively argued that past patterns of collabora-
Experience and   tion between nations will influence their
Mutual Relevance   subsequent behavior, that successful collaboration begets further collaboration, and that
not only past failures but autonomy also leads to further autonomy and
isolationism. In accord with our general model, we offered the hypothesis
that the greater the previous collaboration between two nations, the
greater their subsequent mutual relevance (Proposition 16a). This may
be seen as the result of learned habits and memories of mutual attention
and greater interactive capabilities arising from formal or standardized
procedures established or agreed upon between nations.

Because collaboration can result in frustration and disillusionment as well as satisfaction, we entertained the null hypothesis (Proposition 16b) that past collaboration will have no impact on the level of interaction between nations. In support of this null hypothesis, we may note that cooperation denotes formal governmental agreements, whereas mutual relevance is measured in terms of informal, or nongovernmental, forms of intercourse. It is quite possible that collaboration between governments will have little or no bearing on nongovernmental intercourse. The European Free Trade Association (EFTA), for example, is largely a paper agreement among seven Western European countries; at least it is generally agreed that the EFTA has had little influence on transactions among Western European nations.

In the North Atlantic region, past collaborative experience is measured by the number of agreements in different content areas[1] signed by two or more North Atlantic governments. In relating previous cooperation to mass perceptions, as an indicator of relevance, the relationship between the affective and policy components of mass opinion in 1952 were correlated with various substantive types of collaboration. A correlation matrix is presented in Table 7.1.[2]

All of the product-moment correlations are fairly low, with the highest relationship between cultural pacts and the policy component of

TABLE 7.1

*The Relationship Between Prior Governmental Collaboration
and Opinion Distributions in 1952*

	MIL	LEG	TRAV	CUL	SCI	TOTAL
Affective Component	.13	.14	.13	.02	.06	.08
Policy Component	.09	.05	.12	.22	.15	.03

None of the above correlations is significant at the .05 level. Only those substantive subcomponents of governmental collaboration which have a correlation of at least .10 with either the affective or policy component are included. This excludes political pacts which are correlated with the affective and policy components at .05 and .03 respectively; trade pacts with correlations of .01 and .01 respectively; economic aid pacts at .09 and .01 respectively; and miscellaneous pacts with .08 and .03.

1. Content areas refer to the subdivisions discussed in Chapter 4 (i.e., political, military, trade, etc.).
2. The correlations for the years 1955, 1958, 1961, and 1964 were of similar magnitude (i.e., not significant at the .05 level). For the correlations, see Cobb (1967, Appendix 4).

opinion reaching only .22. The total number of pacts signed, or the summary measure, is correlated with the affective and policy components at only .08 and .03 respectively. This tends to support Proposition 16b that prior cooperation is not salient in developing mutual relevance in terms of attitudinal distributions. In terms of attitudinal integration, neither proximity nor prior integrative experience are that salient in predicting opinion distributions.

The impact of prior collaboration on transactions in 1952 appears in Table 7.2.[3] The data endorse Proposition 16a, as prior collaboration predicts to future interaction with a canonical solution of .70. The variables with the highest loadings at the governmental level are the travel and transportation pacts, with the highest weightings among the criteria for mail and tourism. Governmental pacts which reduce impediments to the free flow of tourism result in even greater tourism. The same pattern is shown in correlating the total number of prior agreements with mail and tourism; product-moment correlations of .51 and .45 respectively are obtained.[4]

TABLE 7.2

The Impact of Prior Governmental Collaboration upon Transactions in 1952

CANONICAL CORRELATION = 0.70

COEFFICIENTS FOR THE FIRST SET OF VARIABLES

Pol	Mil	Trad	Econ-Agr
.03	.15	.02	.30

Leg	Trav	Cul	Sci	Misc
.20	.60	.11	.40	.10

COEFFICIENTS FOR THE SECOND SET OF VARIABLES

Mail	Stud	Telg	Tour	Trad
.70	.03	.35	.45	.13

3. The hypothesis was supported so canonical solutions were not computed for prior collaboration and other time-periods, given the high correlation for 1952 and the high degree of interrelationship among transactions. For the canonical solutions in the North Atlantic study, the BMD 05M program provides several solutions, with only the highest canonical solution presented. In all instances, the first solutions had a much higher coefficient than any of the others. All of the canonical solutions presented in this chapter are significant at the .01 level for the North Atlantic study. For the formula involved in computing the significance level, see Rutherford (1967).

4. Both of these correlations are significant at the .05 level, with a total N of 210 dyads.

Summary Impact of Background Variables.   In assessing the impact of all three sets of background variables (prior collaboration, wartime alignments, and geographic proximity/common boundaries), differential impacts are noted. In looking first at the variables' impact on ensuing attitudinal distributions, the affective component of mass attitudes must be examined. A multiple correlation coefficient for proximity, common boundaries, previous integrative experience, and impact of the war on positive affect in 1952 was .30.[5] There is a slight indication that background factors, when treated as a set, are relevant in explaining ensuing distributions of positive affect.

The multiple correlation coefficient for the impact of the same background factors on the policy component in 1952 is .17.[6] Elements hypothesized to be of some importance account for very little in predicting ensuing policy distributions. In both the affective and the policy components, Propositions 2b, 9b, and 17b are supported, which negates the influence of the background variables studied in predicting opinions when an attitude is used as an indicator of mutual relevance.

In examining the impact of prior elements on transactions, we note a canonical solution of .70 when using only previous collaborative elements. The canonical solution for the impact of background conditions on transactions in 1952 is presented in Table 7.3. The hypothesis (Proposition 16a) asserting the linkage between background conditions and transactions has empirical support with a canonical solution of .80. The largest weights among collaborative variables are pacts concerning travel (.53), with medium weightings for economic aid (.26) and scientific agreements (.29). In addition, the impact of World War II has a fairly sizable loading (.45). In terms of criteria, mail flow has the largest weighting (.64) followed by tourism (.30). Previous agreements concerning travel appear to be linked with ensuing flows of tourists. Secondly, World War II alignments, while having little impact on attitudes, were important in influencing transactions particularly mail flows after a cessation of hostilities. Prior collaborative experience and wartime alignments do tend to predict to ensuing transactional exchange.

A similar result is found in the analysis of the global system. As can be seen from Table 7.4, those dyads with the greatest previous collaboration do tend to show the most mutual relevance, which supports Proposition 16a. The results shown in the table also reveal some rather interesting

5. The correlations were not any larger when examined for the affective component in 1955, 1958, 1961, and 1964. The correlations can be found in Cobb (1967, Appendix 4). In assessing the impact of the background variables, the total number of pacts signed was used as the measure for previous collaboration.
6. The correlations were not any larger for the policy component in 1955, 1958, 1961, and 1964; for the results, see Cobb (1967, Appendix 4).

TABLE 7.3

The Impact of Background Conditions upon Transactions in 1952

CANONICAL CORRELATION $= 0.80$

COEFFICIENTS FOR THE FIRST SET OF VARIABLES

POL	MIL	TRAD	ECON-ARG	LEG		
.06	.18	.04	.26	.19		
TRAV	CUL	SCI	MISC	PROX	CB	WWII
.53	.12	.29	.17	.22	.15	.45

COEFFICIENTS FOR THE SECOND SET OF VARIABLES

MAIL	STUD	TELG	TOUR	TRAD
.64	.14	.14	.30	.10

patterns. Note, for example, in the first canonical solution that trade is the indicator of mutual relevance most influenced by previous collaboration. But it is affected only slightly by formal trade agreements and much more by previous patterns of intergovernmental collaboration in legal matters, transportation, science and technology, and miscellaneous matters.

The second solution, which likewise accounts for substantial behavior, offers another interesting pattern of influence. It seems that nations whose collaboration has tended to be largely along the lines of formal legal agreements and cultural exchange and who have not had much collaboration in terms of transportation and technology tend not to show mutual relevance in terms of trade. The mutual relevance which such nations do show tends to be along the lines of more formal communications (radiograms) and common NGO memberships.

Although indicating a much less pronounced behavioral tendency, the third canonical solution suggests that nations with the greatest military, economic, and cultural collaboration tend to exchange students and have substantial telegraph ties. However, they tend not to manifest mutual relevance along any other dimensions.

The pattern shown in the fourth solution is of relatively little importance, but does indicate that nations with only previous military and economic collaborative experience tend to show mutual relevance only in terms of more impersonal communications (radio messages).

The general conclusions we draw from our analysis of the impact of previous collaborative experience on patterns of mutual relevance are threefold. Firstly, previous collaboration does tend to promote mutual relevance in terms of transactions in both regional and global studies. Second, the primary effect of prior cooperation is manifested through

TABLE 7.4

Previous Collaborative Experience as a Predictor of Mutual Relevance

BIVARIATE CORRELATIONS

Inter-Predictor:

Agreements:	Pol	Mil	Trad	Econ	Legal	Trans	Cult	Tech	Other
Pol	1.00	.41	.08	.46	.50	.42	.35	.31	.35
Mil	.41	1.00	.14	.53	.56	.58	.44	.67	.26
Trad	.08	.14	1.00	.19	.11	.19	.14	.17	.13
Econ	.46	.53	.19	1.00	.61	.55	.51	.40	.46
Legal	.50	.56	.11	.61	1.00	.60	.63	.46	.63
Trans	.42	.58	.19	.55	.60	1.00	.49	.66	.51
Cult	.35	.44	.14	.51	.63	.49	1.00	.40	.62
Tech	.31	.67	.17	.40	.46	.66	.40	1.00	.28
Other	.35	.26	.13	.46	.63	.51	.62	.28	1.00

Predictor-Criterion:

	Mail	Telg	Telp	Telx	Trad	Stud	Tour	NGO
Pol	.17	.25	.16	.19	.29	.25	.16	.35
Mil	.24	.30	.22	.21	.42	.42	.14	.26
Trad	.10	.11	.11	.07	.12	.17	.08	.18
Econ	.16	.25	.19	.33	.35	.37	.13	.37
Legal	.31	.38	.35	.48	.50	.38	.27	.54
Trans	.42	.44	.47	.27	.62	.46	.28	.39
Cult	.18	.24	.21	.34	.32	.31	.20	.44
Tech	.35	.34	.42	.17	.53	.45	.23	.24
Other	.30	.30	.34	.45	.48	.34	.24	.48

CANONICAL SOLUTIONS

First Solution: $Rc_{max} = .73$

Predictor Weightings[a]					Criterion Weightings[a]			
Pol	Mil	Trad	Econ	Legal	Mail	Telg	Telp	Telx
−.01	−.02	.06	−.06	.38	−.01	.11	.20	.12
Trans	Cult	Tech	Other		Trad	Stud	Tour	NGO
.39	−.16	.25	.39		.57	.08	−.15	.32

Second Solution: $Rc_2 = .52$

Predictor Weightings[a]					Criterion Weightings[a]			
Pol	Mil	Trad	Econ	Legal	Mail	Telg	Telp	Telx
.08	−.12	.12	.19	.68	−.08	−.02	−.37	.65
Trans	Cult	Tech	Other		Trad	Stud	Tour	NGO
−.60	.43	−.59	.02		−.53	−.18	.23	.63

Third Solution: $Rc_3 = .33$

Predictor Weightings[a]					Criterion Weightings[a]			
Pol	Mil	Trad	Econ	Legal	Mail	Telg	Telp	Telx
−.22	−.86	−.19	−.55	.69	.27	−.34	−.70	.32

Trans	Cult	Tech	Other		Trad	Stud	Tour	NGO
.29	−.31	.20	.26		.18	−1.10	.08	−.10

Fourth Solution:　$Rc_4 = .24$

Predictor Weightings[a]					Criterion Weightings[a]			
Pol	Mil	Trad	Econ	Legal	Mail	Telg	Telp	Telx
−.76	.48	−.34	.56	−.07	.11	−.49	−.09	−.86
Trans	Cult	Tech	Other		Trad	Stud	Tour	NGO
−.63	−.55	.20	.79		.36	.15	−.32	−.70

Fifth Solution:　　　$Rc_5 = .16$
Sixth Solution:　　　$Rc_6 = .09$
Seventh Solution:　　$Rc_7 = .07$
Eighth Solution:　　　$Rc_8 = .04$

[a] Coefficients are for standardized measures.

patterns of trade, although formal trade agreements, per se, are less important in producing this effect than legal, transportation, and technical collaboration in both regional and global studies. Thirdly, because of the substantial reliance that has been placed on the allegedly positive impact of cultural exchange, we feel compelled to note that cultural collaboration, per se, seems to have a relatively minor and somewhat mixed impact on patterns of relative interaction in both studies.

Mutual Relevance and Subsequent Intergovernmental Collaboration　The final linkage in our model and the last hypothesis to be explored essentially reverse the one that we have just considered. Whereas before we sought to ascertain the relationship between previous collaboration as a predictor and patterns of mutual relevance as a criterion, we now turn the question around to ask what impact relative intercourse has on subsequent patterns of collaboration. Here formal intergovernmental collaboration is seen primarily as a response to needs and demands generated by the relative interaction between two states. Thus, the greater the manifest mutual relevance, the greater the subsequent collaboration (Proposition 17). Etzioni (1967, 35–50) asserted that the transaction impact on governmental collaboration should be more immediate than the reverse situation, since time must pass before agreements go into effect.

In the North Atlantic region, canonical solutions were run between all possible time-periods to determine if transactions have an impact on intergovernmental agreements and the length of the time interval for maximum impact. The optimal solutions are presented in Table 7.5.[7]

The data support Proposition 17, as transactions are highly inter-related with ensuing governmental collaboration with the optimum time-period, which appears to be a decade. The canonicals for three-year intervals vary from .63 to .78. However, the canonicals for six-year and nine-year periods never drop below .72. While this is counter to Etzioni's notion of short-term impact, he does suggest that a more long-term impact is not out of the realm of possibility (1967, 40–41).

Assuming a greater impact over a longer period of time, what are the key variables among the predictors which contribute to an optimal solution? For the personal forms of transactions to have the greatest impact in both nongovernmental and formal forms of collaboration, student exchange and tourism should have the highest weightings among the transactions, or first set of variables. In addition, travel should have a high loading in the collaboration, or second set of variables. Focusing on the nine-year interval between 1952 and 1961 with the highest canonical of .84, the following solution is presented in Table 7.6.

In analyzing the respective weights of each of the components in these clusters of variables, we can determine the contribution of each variable to the solution. In this instance, exchange of people in the forms of tourism and student exchange has the greatest impact on governmental collaboration, taking the form of agreements primarily in the area of travel and transportation. This would support I. Galtung's notion that exchange of people will have greater impact on governmental policies than other forms of exchange because travel makes one receptive to the interests and desires of others and government seeks to reflect mass senti-

TABLE 7.5

Canonical Solutions for the Impact of Transactions on Intergovernmental Collaboration

	1952	1955	1958	1961
1952				
1955	.78			
1958	.84	.63		
1961	.84	.72	.71	

7. No treaty data has been published for 1964–1966.

ments in its collaborative behavior. However, the response is primarily in expanding travel opportunities and removing obstacles to transportation between the countries involved (I. Galtung).[8]

In terms of the reverse pattern, or the impact of treaties on ensuing transactional exchanges, the canonical solutions are not as high regardless of the time period examined. None of the canonicals for any of the three periods rises above .53. Canonicals for the nine-year intervals do not appear above .55. However, there is one canonical which is predictably high. The solution predicting from collaboration in the period between 1958–1960 to transactions in 1964 was .89. This was the period during which the Common Market and Free Trade Association went into effect accompanied by a series of treaty signings. For these organizations to have a maximum impact in the economic sphere, trade and economic agreements should have the highest loadings in the predictor, or first, set of variables and trade the highest loading in the second set of variables. The canonical solution for the effect of collaboration on ensuing transactions is presented in Table 7.7.

In this table, the primary impact is not limited to the economic sphere of trade and economic aid. The highest loadings among the predictors are for agreements regarding trade, travel, and political matters. The highest loadings for the criteria are for travel and tourism. This would support Etzioni's thesis (1965) that the collaboration sur-

TABLE 7.6

*Canonical Solution for the Impact of 1952 Transactions upon
1961 Intergovernmental Collaboration*

CANONICAL CORRELATION = 0.84

COEFFICIENTS FOR THE FIRST SET OF VARIABLES

MAIL	STUD	TELG	TOUR	TRAD
.01	.65	.24	.71	.07

COEFFICIENTS FOR THE SECOND SET OF VARIABLES

POL	MIL	TRAD	ECON-AGR	
.24	.41	.03	.11	
LEG	TRAV	CUL	SCI	MISC
.10	.61	.02	.29	.19

8. Tourism was the key predictor at six-year intervals for both 1952–1958 and 1955–1961. In each period, travel and transportation had the highest loading among the collaborative set. To examine each of the above solutions, see Cobb (1967, Appendix 4).

TABLE 7.7

The Impact of Collaborative Behavior in 1958–1960 upon
Transactions in 1964

CANONICAL CORRELATION = 0.89

COEFFICIENTS FOR THE FIRST SET OF VARIABLES

POL	MIL	TRAD	ECON-AGR	
.26	.02	.39	.13	
LEG	TRAV	CUL	SCI	MISC
.12	.28	.18	.07	.14

COEFFICIENTS FOR THE SECOND SET OF VARIABLES

MAIL	STUD	TELG	TOUR	TRAD
.02	.19	.05	.53	.06

rounding the creation of a supranational organizational structure as in 1958–1960 would be most likely to predict to ensuing transactional exchange. In both situations of mutual influence, immediate or short-run impact does not appear as important as longer time-intervals. In terms of the impact of transactions on ensuing governmental collaboration, the longest time-interval of nine years reflects the greatest impact.

In the global study, the findings on the impact of transactions upon collaboration are similar. Proposition 17 is supported, as can be seen from Table 7.8. The strength of the optimal correlation between the eight indicators of mutual relevance and subsequent intergovernmental collaboration is highly comparable to that found between previous collaborative experience and mutual relevance. The dominant relational pattern is somewhat different, however. The most critical indicators of mutual relevance include not only trade and common NGO memberships but also telex communications. Their influence is manifested most notably in collaborative arrangements regarding inter-nation transportation and to a lesser degree in legal and cultural agreements. It is interesting that trade does not seem to spawn trade agreements, per se, but rather seems to harbinger instrumentally important collaborative transportation agreements. This, in turn, tends to promote further trade.

After the first solution, the predictive power of the canonical solutions decay rather markedly. The most striking thing about the second solution is the relation it suggests between student exchange and military agreements. The strength of the relationship is not impressive, but the pattern it indicates seems to argue that nations with considerable interchange of students, but not of tourists and telex communications, are

TABLE 7.8

Mutual Relevance as a Predictor of Formal Intergovernmental Collaboration

BIVARIATE CORRELATIONS

Predictor-Criterion: Agreements: Behavior	Pol	Mil	Trad	Econ	Legal	Trans	Cult	Tech	Other
Mail	.16	.23	.00	.14	.28	.37	.21	.26	.33
Telg	.25	.27	.02	.13	.34	.37	.21	.25	.33
Telp	.24	.22	−.01	.19	.32	.43	.25	.26	.31
Telx	.33	.16	−.02	.25	.38	.48	.43	.30	.30
Trad	.27	.35	.03	.32	.46	.52	.40	.41	.41
Stud	.22	.37	.02	.22	.37	.39	.26	.40	.32
Tour	.29	.16	.05	.16	.28	.36	.30	.21	.21
NGO	.34	.23	.05	.29	.43	.50	.42	.24	.38

CANONICAL SOLUTIONS

First Solution: $Rc_{max} = .74$

Predictor Weightings[a]

Mail	Telg	Telp	Telx
.01	.02	.01	.35
Trad	Stud	Tour	NGO
.41	.00	.12	.40

Criterion Weightings[a]

Pol	Mil	Trad	Econ	Legal
.09	−.06	−.03	.04	.27
Trans	Cult	Tech	Other	
.47	.28	.08	.19	

Second Solution: $Rc_2 = .36$

Predictor Weightings[a]

Mail	Telg	Telp	Telx
.18	.42	−.07	−.59
Trad	Stud	Tour	NGO
.12	.80	−.51	−.20

Criterion Weightings[a]

Pol	Mil	Trad	Econ	Legal
−.22	.79	.05	−.17	−.18
Trans	Cult	Tech	Other	
−.12	−.45	.22	.46	

Third Solution: $Rc_3 = .23$

Predictor Weightings[a]

Mail	Telg	Telp	Telx
−.33	.91	.33	−.43
Trad	Stud	Tour	NGO
−.80	−.11	.09	.58

Criterion Weightings[a]

Pol	Mil	Trad	Econ	Legal
.67	.47	.18	−.35	.24
Trans	Cult	Tech	Other	
.27	−.52	−.97	.12	

Fourth Solution: $Rc_4 = .19$

Predictor Weightings[a]

Mail	Telg	Telp	Telx
.68	−.29	.86	.09
Trad	Stud	Tour	NGO
−.11	−.56	−.90	.17

Criterion Weightings[a]

Pol	Mil	Trad	Econ	Legal
−.51	−.38	−.36	.21	−.10
Trans	Cult	Tech	Other	
.57	−.34	−.25	.51	

Fifth Solution: $Rc_5 = .17$
Sixth Solution: $Rc_6 = .09$
Seventh Solution: $Rc_7 = .06$
Eighth Solution: $Rc_8 = .01$

[a] Coefficients are for standardized measures.

likely to enter into military agreements and little else. This pattern perhaps most reflects the relations between highly developed and less-
developed nations, at least it seems consistent with the general patterns
shown in our analyses of development and military power. Less-developed nations send numerous students to schools in more powerful and
highly developed nations and also receive substantial military assistance
from these nations.

The behavioral tendencies represented in the third and fourth solutions are of minor importance. The patterns are rather perplexing, but
both seem to suggest that the more constrained the manifest mutual
relevance of two nations, the less their formal collaboration.

On the basis of our analysis, the general conclusion we draw is that
the more extensive and intensive the patterns of mutual relevance between two nations, the more likely they are to enter into formal intergovernmental collaborative agreements. These results, when coupled with
those regarding previous collaborative experience, we take as being generally supportive of the functionalist arguments of E. Haas (1958) and
affirmative evidence for Guetzkow's isolation-collaboration hypotheses
(1957).

Impact of Collaboration on Ensuing Attitudinal Integration.   In
addition to showing the reciprocal influence between transactions and
collaboration, we can ask, Does the creation of treaties have any impact
on mass belief systems? Inglehart (1967, 91–100) asserts that a consequence of supranational organizational activity such as the rise of the
Common Market is increasing attitudinal integration both in good feelings toward others and support of politics promoting regional unity. The
average dyadic perceptions of those with good feeling toward others and
support for unity efforts is shown at three-year intervals in Table 7.9.

In both instances, there was an upward trend in the early days of
community formation up to 1955. Since then there has been a slight
incremental increase in perceptions of friendliness of other nations as
well as support for more regional unity. However, the rate of increase is
slight with perceptions leveling off over the last decade. Deutsch (1967)
is correct in predicting an upward trend in mass opinion, but it occurred
prior to the creation of supranational institutions and was the continua-
tion of a trend in evidence prior to the Treaty of Rome in 1958. Proposition 18b is supported, as attitudes are not noticeably altered by supranational pacts.

Conclusion   In the last three chapters we have reported
the results of an empirical evaluation of the
hypotheses flowing from a general model for the study of internation
collaborative behavior outlined in Chapter 2 and elaborated in Chapter 3.

TABLE 7.9

Average Level of Dyadic Perception of Friendliness of Others and Support for Regional Integration at Five Different Time-Intervals

	1952	1955	1958	1961	1964
Affective Component	46%	52%	55%	55%	57%
Policy Component[1]	53%	60%	63%	62%	63%

[1] The policy component of opinion is the only measure in the study which is not truly dyadic. To make it dyadic, perceptions of unity were applied to all relevant dyads. For example, the percentage of French support for efforts toward achieving Western unity in 1952 would be assigned to all dyads involving Western nations and France.

The findings presented are qualified by data limitations, the sources used, and by the adequacy of the operational measures employed. With this disclaimer, we are fairly confident that the results provide a reasonably accurate theoretical description of the relational patterns among the 1176 global dyads under study in the mid-1950s and 210 North Atlantic dyads over a twelve-year period.

The implications of the findings will be discussed in the next chapter. Our objective was to discover, first, the impact, if any, of a number of background factors on the patterns of relative interaction between nations and, next, how these patterns of mutual relevance relate to subsequent intergovernmental collaboration. The first pattern, geographical factors, were assumed to be related to the material and psychic costs of international intercourse. The economy of interaction with more proximate nations tends to have sway globally, particularly when a common boundary is involved, but not regionally. A second set of background factors involved analytic properties of nation-pairs arising from internal societal traits. The common thread running throughout the analysis was that each societal element was in some way related to a nation's capacity to act. In the global system, three factors, in particular, bore marked resemblance to the mutual relevance manifested by two nations. Homogeneity and level of welfare realization, socioeconomic development, and bureaucratic capabilities led to greater mutual relevance of nation-pairs. A third type of background property, systemic elements, stressed the role of previous collaboration. Patterns of previous treaty alignments tended to show the greatest mutual relevance in both the regional and global systems. Reversing the predictor-criterion relationship to correspond to the last component in our general model, we found that mutual relevance had an impact on subsequent impact of governmental collaboration in both systems. Formal collaboration tends not to represent the

mere institutionalization and/or legitimation of extant patterns of interaction as much as it does a response to the instrumental demands of
transnational intercourse.

In sum, we feel that our general model served well. Perhaps the
most surprising aspect of the findings in terms of the model was the relatively minor role played by most of the societal factors in both systems.
Certainly, considerable mutual relevance can exist in the face of substantial unit heterogeneity.

PART IV

REVIEW AND CONCLUSIONS

chapter 8

Two Levels of Community: A Reappraisal

Introduction   Jacob and Teune have addressed themselves
                  to some of the key problems in studying the
interrelationships of various indicators of integration. They state the
problem as follows:

> We need to know not only that a particular condition or factor has some
> influence upon political behavior, but how much influence it has and in
> what combination it functions with other determinants of integration [3].

An attempt was made to delineate separate measures of cooperation and
determine the extent of their interrelationships. The impact of various
background conditions was evaluated in the fostering of favorable perceptions and cooperation between nations in the North Atlantic area and
the global system. A study employing the dyad as the unit of analysis
was undertaken using geophysical, societal, and systemic properties to
predict patterns of mutual relevance. In the process, propositions regarding indicators of integration were tested and must now be reevaluated
in the perspective of the empirical study. In concluding the investigation,
we will review the major propositions and discuss their implications for
theory and research.

General Overview   In recent years, international relations schol-
                      ars have shown a growing concern for the
conditioning importance of background phenomena, particularly internal

background traits, on the external behavior of nations (Rosenau). Although this concern has come to full bloom only in the more recent literature, it dates at least from a perspicacious article by Guetzkow in 1950. Perhaps the major impetus for work which he envisioned has come from the increasing emphasis on more systematic-oriented research. Whatever its source, this concern now finds its fullest expression in the study of international community and integration.

Consistent with this general orientation, we have detailed a model for the study of inter-nation interaction and collaboration. The basic propositions underlying the model are two: (1) the mutual behavioral relevance exhibited by two nations tends to be a function of three types of background factors (i.e., properties of the geophysical environment, internal societal traits and systemic characteristics); and (2) increasing mutual relevance tends to foster greater intergovernmental collaboration. The mutual relevance of two nations is assumed to be established through, and defined by, relative interaction along eight fairly common indicators of transnational intercourse.

In an effort to measure these various sets of elements, a wide variety of indicators have been used. Geophysical environment was measured by geographic proximity and common boundaries. Internal societal traits included values, attitudinal clusters at the mass level, cultural homogeneity, social welfare values, socioeconomic development, political stability, military power, economic power, bureaucratic capabilities, and common historical experience in terms of war alignments, age, and possession of colonies. Systemic properties referred to previous patterns of treaty alignments. Finally, the eight interaction variables measuring mutual relevance included trade, mail, telex, telegraph, telephone, tourism, student exchange, and common nongovernmental memberships in international nongovernmental organizations.

Summary of Major Findings   The results of an empirical analysis of 1176 pairings of forty-nine nations in the global sample and 210 pairings of fifteen nations in the North Atlantic sample are generally supportive of the model. In abbreviated form, the major findings are listed below.

Mutual Relevance.   There is a positive correlation among the various indicators of mutual relevance in both systems. There are higher correlations among exchanges of communications and goods (trade, mail, telegraph) than among exchanges of people (tourism, student exchange) in the regional study. This pattern is not as pronounced in the global system.

Geophysical Factors.   Geographically more proximate nations tend to show greater mutual relevance in the global system. This tendency is most pronounced when a common boundary is involved. Proximity and common boundaries were not influential in predicting patterns of mutual relevance in the North Atlantic region.

Societal, or Unit, Properties. 1. There is a slight tendency for politically more homogeneous nations to show greater mutual relevance. The weakness of the relationship is the most striking feature of the finding, particularly given its alleged importance. In the regional study, two key attitudes were examined as the equivalent value indicators: the affective and policy aspects. The two were separate measures and not highly correlated. The affective component was more stable than the policy component. Mass attitudes did not predict to ensuing interaction.

2. Culturally more homogeneous nations tend to show somewhat greater mutual relevance in the global system, but the effect is at best a variable set of moderate impact.

3. Nations with common historical attributes in terms of age and general stability but with dissimilar colonial experience show a slight tendency toward greater mutual relevance in the global system. In the North Atlantic system, previous wartime alignments were noteworthy in predicting future interchange particularly mail and tourism.

4. The more homogeneous two nations are in terms of social welfare and the greater their average level of warfare realizations, the more mutually relevant they tend to be in the global system.

5. As homogeneity of two nations with respect to socioeconomic development and average developmental level increases, the greater their relative intercourse in the global system.

6. Militarily more powerful dyads tend to exhibit somewhat greater mutual behavioral relevance in the global system, although the tendency is certainly not a pronounced one.

7. The relative stability of political regimes of two nations and their average duration has little relation to patterns of mutual intercourse in the global system.

8. There is a tendency for economically more powerful dyads to show more mutual relevance in the global system. This tendency is based on realized economic capabilities, not potential capacity.

9. The greater the similarity between two nations in terms of bureaucratic capabilities in the global system, the greater their relative interaction.

Systemic Properties. Previous collaborative experience promotes mutual relevance in both systems, particularly past pacts concerning travel and ensuing tourism in the North Atlantic region.

Intergovernmental Collaboration. The more mutually relevant two nations, the greater their subsequent level of intergovernmental collaboration in both systems. The strongest relation in the North Atlantic region occurred over a time period of more than three years. In addition, collaboration also predicted to greater mutual relevance in both systems. In the North Atlantic region, pacts between 1958–1960 or the period during which the Common Market was created predicted most highly to ensuing transactions. Institutional activity in terms of collaboration did not have a great impact on ensuing mass attitudes in the North Atlantic region, particularly after 1958.

A summary representation of the correlations between the various background factors and behavioral patterns indicating mutual relevance in both systems is presented in Table 8.1.[1] Factors of all three types showed substantial correlation with the eight variables, a composite measure of mutual relevance in the global system. It may be observed from the table that by far the most important societal predictors of mutual relevance were found to be associated with a general developmental syndrome in the global system. We take this finding to be generally consistent with the functionalist theory of international relations, particularly because the influence of previous collaborative experience seems to be fairly diffuse. This finding is further reinforced by the relational pattern found with respect to the final hypothesis flowing from the model. Dyads exhibiting the greatest mutual relevance also tend to show the greatest subsequent intergovernmental collaboration, the best canonical correlation between the two being a fairly heavy .74.

Reevaluation of Integration Theory   There is little doubt that some integration theorists have been too optimistic in assuming a necessary congruence among various integrative indicators. Deutsch (1962, 212–218) assumed that favorable perceptions of other nations and unity efforts were necessarily intertwined. However, in the last fifteen years, in the regional study there has been no overlapping to the extent posited by Deutsch. There has been growth in the amount of cooperation in exchange of items, but there has been no corresponding rise in the affective and policy components. The notion of "congruence" among indicators is not supported, as no underlying process has yet been found to capture the dynamics of various forms of cooperation. Because of this, our suggestion in Chapter 2 that the term be dropped has merit; instead reference should be made to a specific form of cooperation.

Attitudes and Values as Integrative Indicators.   A key notion in the development of cohesion revolves around mass perceptions. No con-

---

1. The relevant variables in the North Atlantic study are proximity, values (salience of key attributes), historical experience (wartime alignment), and previous collaboration.

*Comparison of Predictive Power of Various Background Factors
in Terms of Mutual Relevance in Both Systems*

Optimal Correlation	GEO PROX	POL VALUES	CULT	COM HIST	SOC WEL	DEV	REGIME STAB	MIL POWER	ECON POWER	BUREAU CAP	PREV COL
1.00											
.95											
.90											
.85											
.80											
.75											X
.70											NA
.65						X					
.60	X				X				X		
.55											
.50											
.45											
.40			X	NA					X		
.35								X			
.30		X		X							
.25	NA										
.20		NA									
.15											
.10							X				
.05											
.00											

SOCIETAL PROPERTIES

NA = North Atlantic study; X = global study.

gruence was found between the two indicators of mass attitudes, and the most reliable indicator was found to be perceptions of friendliness toward other nations, which supports the finding concerning the pervasiveness and stability of stereotypes (Scott, 1965, 72–74). An examination of such attitudes reveals more than restlessness and reflects some enduring reaction by a national mass toward other nations.

The importance of certain background factors as determinants of attitudinal distributions has been overplayed. Prior collaboration and wartime alignments have only negligible impact on mass perceptions. Even proximity, which has the strongest tie to attitudes, does not have its alleged strong link. Aspects of governmental policy such as alignments and agreements do not appear to have a bearing on how different peoples will respond to various kinds of integrative symbols.

Transactions as Integrative Indicators. In contrast to the attitudinal findings, a strong relationship was found among the various measures of transactions. This supports the contentions advanced by some theorists that cooperation in one form will be reciprocated in other forms (Deutsch et al., 1957; Etzioni, 1965; Guetzkow, 1957; Russett, 1963).

Another item of particular importance in assessing the adequacy of previous postulates regarding integration is the dichotomy into which all transnational measures are placed. The division between communications exchange, such as mail and telegraph, and human exchange, such as tourism, has been alleged to be of great importance. New cultural experience in terms of student exchange and tourism has been cited as a basis for increasing the level of cooperation. However, these studies indicate that mere interchange is not going to have any lasting impact in and of itself. Either the process by which cooperation in these forms filters to mass perceptions occurs over a longer interval than the span investigated or the link between cooperation and positive affect is much more tenuous than previous findings have indicated.

Importance of Supranational Organizations. Another finding which has not been completely supported is the assumption that the mere creation of supranational organizations and ensuing exchanges deriving therefrom will necessarily lead to more favorable mass perceptions. In Western Europe, the upsurge in mass-opinion positive affect appears to have been primarily before the flurry of supranational activity in the late 1950's, not after. This would tend to indicate that other kinds of elements such as communications exchange might be just as salient in building communities as the creation of more organizations transcending national boundaries. However, further research is required before any summary statements can be made.

In summary, the two measures of attitudes are not highly interrelated. An indication exists that not only are there separate, distinct components of integration but there are also divergent elements within the sphere of mass perceptions. The component of positive affect attributed to others appears to be the most stable of the attitudinal variables with weak linkages to various forms of transactional exchange.

Consequences for Western Europe The empirical research indicates that an international community is a threshold phenomenon. If one is arguing that there must be high degrees of cooperation and overwhelming mass support for unity efforts, then such a situation has not appeared in the North Atlantic area and prospects appear dim for the near future. If more lenient criteria are used such as increasing transactional exchange and a base of mass support, then Western Europe could be classified as integrated. Deutsch's ultimate objective of an amalgamated security community, or union, is unlikely to be achieved, since a continual upswing in attributions of positive affect and support for unity efforts is required. However, a more viable alternative is the pluralistic security community where conflicts are settled peacefully. There is a basis for mutual cooperation in the North Atlantic area, but unity in an ultimate form is far removed from the contemporary scene.

Another consideration is the relevance of attitudinal measures as indicators of cohesion. The extent of positive affect distributed among national masses does not reflect the collaborative atmosphere existing in terms of the propensity to transact. Perhaps a more important element in terms of short-run payoffs is elite attitudes or how decision-makers change their attitudes over time as an indicator of how collaboration expands in a particular area. An alternative explanation is that integration, if defined in terms of an expansive popular commitment to collaborative activity, can develop only after the passage of several decades given an effective supranational organization. This may be the final stage on a continuum evincing different degrees of cohesion, and only successful completion of transactional interaction over time can permit such a popular receptivity to occur.

In addition, the process may reflect more of an ebb-and-flow than a unilinear progression to an ultimate state of unification. An alternative explanation gives some support to Burton's thesis questioning the salience of "internationalization." Concerning the impact of supranational organs on mass attitudes, Burton could argue that an ultimate state of amalgamation is far removed; the activities of such organs are not as far-reaching in their impact as might be imagined. As a substitute for supranationalism, the primacy of domestic matters may be the hallmark of the coming decades and efforts toward regional cohesion will not be as salient as in the past (Burton, 55–66). However, one could not argue for this extreme given either the high levels of responsiveness on transactional exchange or intergovernmental collaboration as demonstrated in this study. As a consequence, the European attempt at community formation falls somewhere between the extreme of impotence argued by Burton and the complete congruence of all indicators argued by Deutsch (1960a).

Consequences for the Global System   Bearing in mind the exploratory nature of the study and the tentativeness of its findings, some results seem sufficiently relevant to merit observation. First, the relatively low correlations we obtained between patterns of mutual relevance and common political values, cultural homogeneity and common historical attributes, indicates that fairly intense relations can exist despite substantial heterogeneity in terms of values, interests, and perspectives. Nations can be tolerant of considerable diversity in relations with one another.

The most important internal factor promoting intensive behavioral ties between nations is the general socioeconomic and political development of a nation. This suggests that if our goal is to build some form of world community, there are more than just humanitarian and Cold War reasons for the more developed nations to aid their less-developed neighbors in attempting to modernize.

Finally, the observed relationships between patterns of mutual relevance and both previous and subsequent collaboration suggest that neither military nor cultural exchange agreements are very effective in promoting mutual relevance between nations. In many ways, Morgenthau (1960, 519) may be correct in downgrading the importance of what he terms the "cultural approach" to world community. Rather than military and/or cultural agreements, what appears to be needed are more functional forms of collaboration and intercourse.

Suggestions for Further Research   The research that has been reported must be considered groundwork for more sophisticated elaboration. Each of the hypotheses explored is deserving of more detailed and careful scrutiny, both in the aggregate and disaggregated forms of analysis. We have examined continuous as opposed to contingent relationships. The possibilities of step functions or threshold effects certainly need to be investigated.

Following a strategy outlined by Guetzkow (1950) nearly two decades ago, we have tried to provide the crude beginnings of a general binary theory of international interaction and collaboration. We are convinced that developments along these lines can be a substantial improvement over the prevailing monadic orientation. But, at the same time, we must not limit ourselves to relatively simple binary systems; consideration must be given to larger and more complex systems. The development of more adequate means for the rigorous treatment of multiple bondings is a major methodological challenge to students of international relations.

In assessing future directions which will be taken in research on the nature and extent of cohesion achieved by nation-states, a number of possibilities exist within the context of this study. In an attempt to search for generalizations which are applicable to all dyads, little attention was paid to individual nation-pairs. However, the utility of this technique has been demonstrated and might provide a further insight (Russett, 1963). For example, the British–French dyad runs counter to many of the findings which were applicable to most dyads in the North Atlantic study. Transaction exchange rates have not increased, and attitudinal perceptions of each other have become less friendly with the passage of time. The lack of responsiveness might be related to current policy disagreements between the two governments or to background factors which were germinating prior to the presence of key decision-makers such as de Gaulle. The prospects for further regional cohesion could be assessed given a cleavage between two key countries in the region. Intensive case studies on more measures than discussed in this study might be related to the more general phenomenon of the likelihood of further policy rifts in an area.

Similarly, West Germany and France could be viewed as a case study in a successful dyadic relationship which has become more responsive with the passage of time. High rates of transactional exchange and reciprocal positive perceptions are even more spectacular in this situation, where the prospects of achieving a pluralistic security community were dim fifteen years ago. An effort could be made to determine what key elements in either the transactional or attitudinal indicators of integration served as harbingers of the development of cooperative bonds, given a disruptive history with both in opposing camps during the Second World War.

Another focus for analysis in future studies would be the extent to which the findings in the North Atlantic area are generalizable to other regions. Are the notions regarding the interrelationship of transactional indicators subject to only one region? Perhaps Western Europe is a unique case reflecting a superordinate degree of cultural homogeneity and a highly industrialized stage of economic development. Studies of Latin America, Southeast Asia, and Africa would be needed to determine the extent to which the different indicators of regional cohesion used in this study are consistent with our North Atlantic findings.

Another focus requiring further study is an examination of different units of analysis. Directional and summed dyads are not the only forms of summing nation interaction. A focus on the triad or larger numbers of nations would provide additional theoretical leverage. One could investigate the primacy of certain countries and whether a particular nation serves as a focus for all interactions (Brams, 1965). Singer (1963, 420–430) asserts that there is a need to examine not only dyadic reciprocity within the international system but the interplay of several states as well.

A greater number of longitudinal studies is needed at the global level in particular. A key is data availability in all of the proposed efforts. Nonetheless, we are obliged to avail ourselves of information which is available, a supply which is considerably more ample than is commonly supposed. Fault can be found with these data and their sources; but to dismiss such efforts as inadequate is a hasty conclusion. Quantifiable information can surely carry us further toward the development of sound empirical theory than plaintive cries of exasperation and despair. Every effort should be made to obtain even more adequate data. There can be little doubt that if our qualms about data are reflected in qualifications regarding the results of analysis, we will be much further along than if we allow them to stifle empirical inquiry.

Conclusion   If, in closing, we may be permitted to venture beyond the scope of our study and rather freely extrapolate our findings, we see little to indicate any form of amalgamated world community in the offing. Nor, for that matter, do we think that such a community would necessarily be desirable. A more limited objective would be relevant to our expectations. Perhaps the best hope is the community envisioned by Burton, a series of interdependent but relatively autonomous nations, a community predicated on a mutual respect for the independence and integrity of all. Such a community will not be founded by any cutting of the Gordian knot, but rather through the painfullly slow processes of developing functional interests and capacities for mutually responsive action. We are not particularly dismayed by Deutsch's finding (1961) that there has been a relative decline in international life in comparison to domestic activities. The important thing is that international life has continued to grow. Save one foul problem, time may be on our side.

Bibliography

INTEGRATION LITERATURE

Abrams, M. "British Elite Attitudes and the European Common Market." *Public Opinion Quarterly,* **20,** 236–246, 1965.

Ake, C. "Political Integration and Political Stability." *World Politics,* **19,** 486–499, 1967.

Almond, G. *The American People and Foreign Policy.* New York: Praeger, 1960.

Angell, R. "The Growth of Transnational Participation." *Journal of Social Issues,* **23,** 108–129, 1967.

Beloff, J. "Britain, Europe and the Atlantic Community." In F. Wilcox and H. F. Haviland (Eds.), *The Atlantic Community.* New York: Praeger, 1963.

Blau, P. and W. Scott. *Formal Organizations.* San Francisco: Chandler, 1962.

Boulding, K. "National Images and International Systems." *Journal of Conflict Resolution,* **3,** 120–131, 1959.

Brams, S. "Flow and Form in the International System." Ph.D. dissertation, Department of Political Science, Northwestern University, August, 1965.

Brams, S. "Transaction Flows in the International System." *American Political Science Review,* **60,** 880–898, 1966.

Brams, S. "A Note on the Cosmopolitanism of World Regions." Paper presented at the 1967 meeting of the Mid-West Political Science Association, Lafayette, Indiana, April 1967.

Brody, R. "Some Systemic Effects of the Spread of Nuclear Weapons Technology: A Study Through Simulation of a Multi-Nuclear Future." *Journal of Conflict Resolution*, **7**, 665–753, 1963.

Buchanan, W. and H. Cantril. *How Nations See Each Other*. Urbana: University of Illinois Press, 1953.

Burton, J. *International Relations*. Cambridge, United Kingdom: Cambridge University Press, 1965.

Cobb, R. "The Use of Mass Opinion and Transactions as Indicators of Integration: A Study of the North Atlantic Area." Ph.D. dissertation, Department of Political Science, Northwestern University, August 1967.

Coser, L. *The Functions of Social Conflict*. New York: Free Press, 1961.

Davis, K. "Social Change Affecting International Relations." In J. Rosenau (Ed.), *International Politics and Foreign Policy*. New York: Free Press, 1961.

Davison, W. *International Political Communication*. New York: Praeger, 1965.

Deutsch, K. *Political Community at the International Level: Problems of Definition and Measurement*. Garden City: Doubleday, 1954.

Deutsch, K. "The Propensity to International Transactions." *Political Studies*, **8**, 147–155, 1960a.

Deutsch, K. "Toward an Inventory of Basic Trends and Patterns in Comparative and International Politics." *American Political Science Review*, **54**, 34–57, 1960b.

Deutsch, K. "Supranational Organizations in the 1960's." *Journal of Common Market Studies*, **1**, 212–218, 1962.

Deutsch, K. *Nerves of Government*. New York: Free Press, 1963.

Deutsch, K. "Communication Theory and Political Integration." In P. Jacob and J. Toscano (Eds.), *The Integration of Political Communities*. Philadelphia: Lippincott, 1964a.

Deutsch, K. "Transaction Flows as Indicators of Political Cohesion." In P. Jacob and J. Toscano (Eds.), *The Integration of Political Communities*, Philadelphia: Lippincott, 1964b.

Deutsch, K. *Nationalism and Social Communication*. Cambridge: MIT Press, 1966.

Deutsch, K., S. Burrell, R. Kann, M. Lee, M. Lichterman, R. Lindgren, F. Loewenheim, R. Van Wagenen. *Political Community and the North Atlantic Area*. Princeton: Princeton University Press, 1957.

Deutsch, K. and L. Edinger. *Germany Rejoins the Powers*. Stanford: Stanford University Press, 1959.

Deutsch, K., L. Edinger, R. Macridis, and R. Merritt. *France, Germany and the Western Alliance*. New York: Scribners, 1967.

Deutsch, K. and W. Isard. "A Note on a Generalized Concept of Effective Distance." *Behavioral Science*, **6**, 308–311, 1961.

Deutsch, K. and R. Merritt. "Effect of Events on International Images." In H. Kelman (Ed.), *International Behavior*. New York: Holt, 1965.

Deutsch, K. and R. Savage. "A Statistical Model of the Gross Analysis of Transaction Flows." *Econometrika,* **28,** 551–572, 1960.

Elder, C. "An Empirical Study of Some Background Conditions of Inter-Nation Collaboration." Ph.D. dissertation, Department of Political Science, Northwestern University, June 1970.

Emerson, R. "Pan-Africanism." *International Organization,* **16,** 275–290, 1962.

Etzioni, A. "European Unification: A Strategy of Change." *World Politics,* **16,** 32–51, 1963.

Etzioni, A. *Political Unification.* New York: Holt, 1965.

Etzioni, A. *Studies in Social Change.* New York: Holt, 1966.

Gallup International. "Public Opinion and the European Community." *Journal of Common Market Studies,* **2,** 101–126, 1963.

Galtung, I. "The Impact of Study Abroad." *Journal of Peace Research,* **3,** 258–275, 1965.

Galtung, J. "Pacifism from a Sociological Point of View." *Journal of Conflict Resolution,* **3,** 67–84, 1959.

Galtung, J. "East-West Interaction Patterns." *Journal of Peace Research,* **4,** 146–177, 1966.

Gamson, W. and A. Modigliani. "Knowledge and Foreign Policy Considerations." *Public Opinion Quarterly,* **31,** 187–199, 1966.

Gordon, L. "Economic Regionalism Reconsidered." *World Politics,* **13,** 231–253, 1961.

Guetzkow, H. "Long-Range Research in International Relations." *American Perspective,* **4,** 421–440, 1950.

Guetzkow, H. "Isolation and Collaboration: A Partial Theory of International Relations." *Journal of Conflict Resolution,* **1,** 46–68, 1957.

Haas, E. *The Uniting of Europe.* Stanford: Stanford University Press, 1958.

Haas, E. "International Integration: The European and the Universal Process." *International Organization,* **15,** 366–392, 1961.

Haas, E. *Beyond the Nation-State.* Stanford: Stanford University Press, 1966.

Haas, E. and P. Schmitter. "Economics and Differential Patterns of Political Integration: Projections About Unity in Latin America." In *International Political Communication.* Garden Ctiy: Anchor, 1966.

Hoffman, S. "International Relations: The Long Road to Theory." *World Politics,* **11,** 346–377, 1959.

Hoffman, S. "Discord in Community: The North Atlantic Area as a Partial International System." *International Organization,* **17,** 521–549, 1963.

Homans, G. *Social Behavior.* New York: Harcourt, 1961.

Inglehart, R. "An End to European Integration?" *American Political Science Review,* **61,** 91–105, 1967.

Inglehart, R. "Trends and Non-Trends in the Western Alliance: A Review." *Journal of Conflict Resolution,* **12,** 120–128, 1968.

Jacob, P. "The Influence of Values in Political Integration." In P. Jacob and J. Toscano (Eds.), *The Integration of Political Communities.* Philadelphia: Lippincott, 1964.

Jacob, H. and H. Teune. "The Integrative Process: Guidelines for Analyses of the Bases of Political Integration." In P. Jacob and J. Toscano (Eds.), *The Integration of Political Communities.* Philadelphia: Lippincott, 1964.

Kann, R. *The Hapsburg Empire.* New York: Praeger, 1957.

Kaplan, M. *System and Process in International Politics.* New York: Wiley, 1957.

Kelman, H. "Societal, Attitudinal and Structural Factors in International Relations." *Journal of Social Issues,* 11, 42–56, 1953.

Kelman, H. "Socio-psychological Approaches to the Study of International Relations: The Question of Relevance." In H. Kelman (Ed.), *International Behavior.* New York: Holt, 1965.

Key, V. O. *Public Opinion and American Democracy.* New York: Knopf, 1961.

Klineberg, O. *The Human Dimension in International Relations.* New York: Holt, 1965.

Kreisberg, L. "German Public Opinion and The European Coal and Steel Community." *Public Opinion Quarterly,* 23, 28–42, 1959.

Lerner, D. "French Business Leaders Look at EDC," *Public Opinion Quarterly,* 20, 212–221, 1956.

Lerner, D. *The Passing of Traditional Society.* New York: Free Press, 1958.

Levi, W. "The Concept of Integration in Research on Peace." *Background,* 9, 111–126, 1965.

Lewin, K. *Field Theory in Social Science.* Edited by D. Cartwright. New York: Harper, 1951.

Lijphart, A. "Tourist Traffic and Integration Potential." *Journal of Common Market Studies,* 3, 251–262, 1964.

Lindberg, L. *The Political Dynamics of European Economic Integration.* Stanford: Stanford University Press, 1963.

Lindgren, R. *Norway-Sweden.* Princeton: Princeton University Press, 1959.

Linnemann, H. *An Econometric Study of International Trade Flows.* Amsterdam: North Holland Publishing Company, 1966.

Lipset, S. *Political Man.* Garden City: Anchor, 1963.

Liska, G. *International Equilibrium: A Theoretical Essay on the Politics and Organization of Security.* Cambridge: Harvard University Press, 1957.

Liska, G. *Nations in Alliance: The Limits of Interdependence.* Baltimore: Johns Hopkins, 1962.

Lowell, A. *Public Opinion in War and Peace.* Cambridge: Harvard University Press, 1923.

March, J. and H. Simon with H. Guetzkow. *Organizations.* New York: Wiley, 1958.

McClelland, C. "Applications of General Systems Theory in International Relations." *Main Currents in Modern Thought,* 12, 27–34, 1955.

McClelland, C. "Systems and History in International Relations: Some Perspectives for Empirical Research and Theory." *General Systems Yearbook,* 3, 222–234, 1958.

McClelland, C. *Theory and the International System.* New York: Macmillan, 1966.

Meier, R. *A Communications Theory of Urban Growth.* Cambridge: Harvard University Press, 1962.

Merritt, R. "Distance and Interaction Among Political Communities." *General Systems Yearbook,* **9,** 255–263, 1964.

Merritt, R. *Symbols of American Community: 1735–1775.* New Haven: Yale University Press, 1966.

Morgenthau, H. "Alliances in Theory and Practice." In A. Wolfers (Ed.), *Alliance Policy in the Cold War.* Baltimore: Johns Hopkins, 1959.

Morgenthau, H. *Politics Among Nations: The Struggle for Power and Peace.* 4th edition, New York: Knopf, 1967.

Nye, J. "East African Economic Integration." In *International Political Communities.* Garden City: Anchor, 1966.

Organski, A. *World Politics.* New York: Knopf, 1958.

Pool, I. "Effects of Cross-National Contact on National and International Images." In H. Kelman (Ed.), *International Behavior.* New York: Holt, 1965.

Pool, I., S. Keller, and R. Bauer. "The Influence of Foreign Travel on Political Attitudes of American Businessmen." *Public Opinion Quarterly,* **20,** 161–175, 1956.

Povolny, M. "Africa in Search of Unity: Model and Reality." *Background,* **9,** 297–318, 1966.

Puchala, D. "European Political Integration: Progress and Prospects." Mimeograph, Department of Political Science, Yale University, 1966.

Queener, L. "The Development of Internationalist Attitudes: Hypotheses and Verifications." *The Journal of Social Psychology,* **29,** 221–235, 1949.

Reigrotski, E. and N. Anderson. "National Stereotypes and Foreign Contacts." *Public Opinion Quarterly,* **23,** 515–528, 1960.

Richardson, J. "The Concept of Atlantic Community." *Journal of Common Market Studies,* **3,** 1–22, 1964.

Rosecrance, R. *Action and Reaction in World Politics: International Systems in Perspective.* Boston: Little, 1963.

Rosenau, J. "Pre-theories and Theories of Foreign Policy." In R. B. Farrell (Ed.), *Approaches to Comparative and International Politics.* Evanston: Northwestern University Press, 1966.

Rummel, R. "The Dimensions of Conflict Behavior Within and Between Nations." *Yearbook of the Society for General Systems Research,* **8,** 1–49, 1963.

Rummel, R. "A Field Theory of Social Action with Application to Conflict Within Nations." *General Systems Yearbook,* **10,** 183–211, 1965.

Rummel, R. "Some Dimensions on the Foreign Behavior of Nations." *Journal of Peace Research,* **3,** 201–221, 1966a.

Rummel, R. "The Dimensionality of Nations Project." In R. Merritt and S. Rokkan (Eds.), *Comparing Nations: The Use of Quantitative Data in Cross-National Research.* New Haven: Yale University Press, 1966b.

Rummel, R. "The Relationship Between National Attributes and Foreign Conflict Behavior." In J. D. Singer (Ed.), *Quantitative International Politics*. New York: Free Press, 1968.

Russett, B. *Community and Contention: Britain and America in the Twentieth Century*. Cambridge: MIT Press, 1963.

Russett, B. *Trends in World Politics*. New York: Macmillan, 1965.

Schokking, J. and N. Anderson. "Observations on the European Integration Precess." *Journal of Conflict Resolution*, 4, 385–410, 1960.

Scott, W. "Psychological and Social Correlates of International Images." In H. Kelman (Ed.), *International Behavior*. New York: Holt, 1965.

Scott, W. "Some Bases for Consistent Attitudes Toward Nations." Paper presented at the 1967 meeting of the American Political Science Association, New York, September, 1966.

Scott, W. and S. Withey. *The United States and the United Nations*. New York: Manhattan, 1958.

Simon, M. *Communist System Interaction with the Developing States: 1954–1962*. Stanford: Stanford Studies of the Communist System, 1966.

Singer, J. D. "The Level of Analysis Problem in International Politics." *World Politics*, 14, 77–92, 1961.

Singer, J. D. "Inter-Nation Influence: A Formal Model." *American Political Science Review*, 57, 420–430, 1963.

Singer, J. D. and M. Small. "Formal Alliances: 1815–1949." *Journal of Peace Research*, 1, 1–32, 1966.

Snyder, R. "Recent Trends in International Relations Theory and Research." In A. Ranney (Ed.), *Essays on the Behavioral Study of Politics*. Urbana: University of Illinois Press, 1962.

Snyder, R., H. Bruck, and B. Sapin. "Decision-Making as an Approach to the Study of International Politics." In R. Snyder, H. Bruck, and B. Sapin (Eds.), *Foreign Policy Decision-Making*. New York: Free Press, 1962.

Snyder, R. and J. Robinson. *National and International Decision-Making*. New York: The Institute for International Order, 1961.

Sondermann, F. "The Linkage Between Foreign Policy and International Politics." In J. Rosenau (Ed.), *International Politics and Foreign Policy*. New York: Free Press, 1961.

Smoker, P. "A Preliminary Empirical Study of an International Integrative Subsystem." *International Association*, 11, 638–646, 1965.

Smoker, P. "International Processes Simulation." Mimeograph, Simulated International Processes Project, Evanston, Illinois, 1967.

Spanier, J. *World Politics In An Age of Revolution*. New York: Praeger, 1967.

Sprout, H. and M. Sprout. "Environmental Factors in the Study of International Politics." *Journal of Conflict Resolution*, 1, 309–328, 1957.

Sprout, H. and M. Sprout. *Man-Milieu Relationship Hypotheses in the Context of International Politics*. Princeton: Princeton University Press, 1956.

Starke, J. *An Introduction to International Law*. London: Butterworth, 1950.

Tanter, R. "A Systems Analysis Guide for Testing Theories of International Political Development." Paper delivered at the 1966 meeting of the American Political Science Association, New York, September, 1966.

Teune, H. "The Learning of Integrative Habits." In P. Jacob and J. Toscano (Eds.), *The Integration of Political Communities.* Philadelphia: Lippincott, 1964.

Toscano, J. "Transaction Flow Analysis in Metropolitan Areas." In P. Jacob and J. Toscano (Eds.), *The Integration of Political Communities.* Philadelphia: Lippincott, 1964.

White, L. "Peace by Pieces: The Role of Non-governmental Organizations." *Annals of the American Academy of Political and Social Science,* 87–97, 1949.

Wolfers, A. "Stresses and Strains in 'Going it with Others'." In A. Wolfers (Ed.), *Alliance Policy in the Cold War.* Baltimore: Johns Hopkins, 1959.

Wright, Q. *The Study of International Relations.* New York: Appleton, 1955.

Wright, Q. *A Study of War.* 2d edition. Chicago: University of Chicago Press, 1965.

METHODOLOGICAL LITERATURE

Anderson, T. *An Introduction to Multivariate Statistical Analysis.* New York: Wiley, 1958.

Cooley, W. and P. Lohnes. *Multivariate Procedures for the Behavioral Sciences.* New York: Wiley, 1963.

Goodman, L. "A Short Computer Program for the Analysis of Transaction Flows." *Behavioral Science,* 9, 176–185, 1964.

Haas, M. "Aggregate Analysis." *World Politics,* 19, 106–121, 1966.

Health Sciences Computing Facility. *Biomedical Computer Programs.* Los Angeles: University of California, 1964.

Hotelling, H. "The Most Predictable Criterion." *Journal of Educational Psychology,* 26, 139–142, 1935.

Koons, P. "Canonical Analysis." In H. Borko (Ed.), *Computer Applications in the Behavioral Sciences.* Englewood Cliffs: Prentice Hall, 1962.

McKeon, J. "Canonical Analysis: Some Relations Between Canonical Correlation, Factor Analysis, Discriminant Function Analysis and Scaling Theory." Mimeograph, Department of Psychology, University of Illinois, 1962.

McNemar, Q. *Psychological Statistics,* 3d edition. New York: Wiley, 1962.

Pool, I., R. Abelson, and S. Popkin. *Candidates, Issues and Strategies.* Cambridge: MIT Press, 1965.

Rao, C. *Advanced Statistical Methods in Biometric Research.* New York: Wiley, 1952.

Rohn, P. "The UN Treaty Series Project as Computerized Jurisprudence." *Texas International Law Forum,* 1, 167–173, 1966.

Rutherford, B. "Canonical Correlation in Political Analysis." Mimeograph, Department of Political Science, Northwestern University, 1967.

DATA SOURCES

Banks, A. and R. Textor. *A Cross-Polity Survey*. Cambridge: MIT Press, 1963.

Biscoe, R. "Social Science Data Archives: A Review of Developments." *American Political Science Review*, **60**, 93–109, 1966.

Encyclopedia Britannica. *World Atlas*. Chicago: World Atlas, 1963.

Gallup Institute. Public opinion polls. Toronto: Gallup Institute of Canada, various years.

Gallup Institute. Public opinion polls. Copenhagen: Gallup Institute of Denmark, various years.

Gallup Institute. Public opinion polls. Oslo: Gallup Institute of Norway, various years.

Gallup Institute. Public opinion polls. Princeton: Gallup Institute of the United States, various years.

Galtung, J. Oslo: International Peace Research Institute.

Government of Australia. Postmaster-General's Department, Melbourne, Australia.

Government of Austria. Ministry of Communications and Electricity, Vienna, Austria.

Government of Belgium. Ministry of Posts, Telegraph, and Telephones, Brussels, Belgium.

Government of Canada. Public Relations Division of the Post Office, Ottawa, Canada.

Government of Chile. Department de Estudios, Santiago, Chile.

Government of Denmark. Ministry of Transport and Public Works, Copenhagen, Denmark.

Government of Finland. Ministry of Communications, Helsinki, Finland.

Government of France. Ministry of Posts and Telecommunications, Paris, France.

Government of the German Federal Republic. Ministry of Posts, Bonn, German Federal Republic.

Government of Israel. Ministry of Posts, Jerusalem, Israel.

Government of Italy. Ministry of Posts and Telegraph, Rome, Italy.

Government of the Netherlands. Ministry of Transport and Waterways, Amsterdam, the Netherlands.

Government of New Zealand. General Post Office, Public Relations Division, Wellington, New Zealand.

Government of Norway. Ministry of Communications, Oslo, Norway.

Government of Panama. Ministerio de Govierno y Justicia, Panama City, Panama.

Government of Spain. Ministry of Information and Tourism, Madrid, Spain.

Government of Sweden. Ministry of Communications, Stockholm, Sweden.

Government of Switzerland. Ministry of Communication, Berne, Switzerland.

Government of Thailand. Ministry of Posts and Telegraph, Bangkok, Thailand.

Government of the United Kingdom. Postmaster General, London, United Kingdom.

Government of the United States. Public Relations Division of the Post Office, Washington, D.C.

Hammond's Company. *Hammond's Standard World Atlas.* New York: Hammond's Company, 1953.

Hastings, P. "The Roper Center: An International Archive of Sample Survey Data." *Public Opinion Quarterly,* 27, 590–598, 1963.

Institute for Marketing. Public opinion polls. Vienna, Austria: Institute for Marketing, various years.

International Air Transport Association. *Tabulation of Great Circle Distances.* Montreal: International Air Transport Association, 1959.

International Labor Organization. *Yearbook of Labor Statistics.* Geneva: International Labor Organization, various years.

International Monetary Fund and International Bank for Reconstruction and Development. *Direction of Trade, Annual 1958–1962.* Washington, D. C.: International Monetary Fund, 1964.

International Telecommunications Union. *General Plan for the Development of the International Network, 1958–1962.* Geneva: International Telecommunications Union, 1964a.

International Telecommunications Union. *General Plan for the Development of the International Network, 1963–1968.* Geneva: International Telecommunications Union, 1964b.

International Telecommunications Union. *General Telegram Statistics.* Geneva: International Telecommunications Union, various years.

International Telecommunications Union. *General Telephone Statistics.* Geneva: International Telecommunications Union, various years.

International Telecommunications. *Telecommunications Journal.* Geneva: International Telecommunications Union, various years.

International Telecommunications Union. *Telex Statistics.* Geneva: International Telecommunications Union, various years.

International Union of Official Travel Organizations. *International Travel Statistics.* Geneva: International Union of Official Travel Organizations, various years.

Merritt, R. and D. Puchala. (Eds.), *Western European Perspectives on International Affairs: Public Opinion Studies and Evaluations.* New York: Praeger, 1967.

National Opinion Research Center. Public opinion polls. Chicago: National Opinion Research Center, various years.

Netherlands Institute of Public Opinion. Public opinion polls. Amsterdam: Netherlands Institute of Public Opinion, various years.

Odyssey Books. *The Odyssey World Atlas.* New York: Odyssey, 1966.

Public Opinion of Belgium. Public opinion polls. Brussels: Public Institute of Belgium, various years.

Rand McNally. *Commercial Atlas and Marketing Guide.* 95th edition. Chicago: Rand McNally, 1964.

Rummel, R. "The Dimensionality of Nations Project: Variable Definitions, Data Sources and Year." Mimeograph, Northwestern University, 1964.

Rummel, R., H. Guetzkow, J. Sawyer, and R. Tanter. *The Dimensionality of Nations.* Forthcoming, 1970.

Russett, B., H. Alker, K. Deutsch, and H. Lasswell. *World Handbook of Political and Social Indicators.* New Haven: Yale University Press, 1964.

Smoker, P. Simulated International Processes Project. Evanston, Ill.; and Lancaster, United Kingdom.

Steinberg, S. (Ed.) *The Statesman's Yearbook.* London: Macmillan, various years.

Union of International Associations. *The Yearbook of International Organizations.* Brussels: Union of International Associations, 1964.

Union Postale Universelle. *Statistique des expeditions dans le service postal international.* Berne: Bureau international De L' Union Postale Universelle, various years.

United Nations. *Demographic Yearbook.* New York: United Nations, various years.

United Nations. *Direction of International Trade, 1950–1958. Statistical Papers, Series T.* New York: United Nations, 1958.

United Nations. *Statistical Yearbook.* New York: United Nations, various years.

United Nations. *Treaty Series, Cumulative Index.* New York: United Nations, 1966.

United Nations Educational, Scientific and Cultural Organization. *Study Abroad.* Paris: United Nations Educational, Scientific and Cultural Organization, various years.

United Nations Educational, Scientific and Cultural Organization. *UNESCO Yearbook.* Paris: United Nations Educational, Scientific and Cultural Organization, various years.

United Nations Information Agency. *Public Opinion in Spain: Comparative Standing of the US versus the USSR* Washington, D. C.: United States Information Agency Research and Reference Service, 1960.

United States Information Agency. *Attitudes Toward the Common Market in Western Europe.* Washington, D. C.: United States Information Agency Research and Reference Service, 1965.

Author Index

f=footnote

Smoker, P., 75
Snyder, R., 7, 16, 61
Sondermann, F., 6
Spanier, J., 3, 35
Sprout, H., 6
Sprout, M., 6
Starke, F., 50 f, 71, 72

Teune, H., 13, 18, 25, 27, 29, 30,
   48, 49, 73, 133

Textor, R., 64, 69, 71
Toscano, J., 8

Wiener, N., 8
Withey, S., 34
Wolfers, A., 27, 45, 46
Wright, P., 10, 15, 16, 17

Zipf, G., 26, 28

Subject Index

alliance, Central African Customs Union, 46
  Central American Common Market, 29, 44
  Common Market, 3, 17, 31, 32, 48, 53, 60, 125, 128
  East African Common Market, 44
  European Coal and Steel Community, 32
  European Defense Community, 33
  European Economic Community, 3, 46
  European Free Trade Association, 118, 125
  Federation of West Indies, 42
  Latin American Free Trade Association, 46
  military, 3, 32
  multilateral, 3
  North Atlantic Treaty Organization, 3, 29
  United Nations, 34
Amalgamated Security Community, 14, 47, 139

analysis, canonical correlation, 78–81
  General Systems, 5
  of transaction flows, 7
  time cuts used for, 77
attributes, 69
attitudes, as indicators, 54
  collaboration and, 128
  institutional impact of, 53
  internal political, 28, 29
  mass, 16, 31(fn)
    policy component of, 67, 68
    stability in, 33–35, 95, 96
    transactions and, 36, 96, 98
  mutual responsiveness and, 18
  proximity and, 88, 119

Central Limit Theorem, 80
cohesion, amount of, 14, 15
  attempts to achieve, 37
  attitudes as indicators of, 139
  basis of political, 14
  magnitude of, 17, 18
  mass perceptions and, 136